On Jim Corbett's Trail

On Jim Corbett's Trail
and Other Tales from Tree-tops

A. J. T. JOHNSINGH

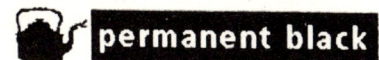

permanent black

Published by

PERMANENT BLACK
D-28, Oxford Apartments, 11 I.P. Extension,
Delhi 110092

Distributed by

ORIENT LONGMAN PRIVATE LTD
Bangalore Bhopal Bhubaneshwar Chandigarh Chennai
Ernakulam Guwahati Hyderabad Jaipur Kolkata
Lucknow Mumbai New Delhi Patna

ISBN 81-7824-081-5

Typeset in AGaramond by Eleven Arts, Delhi 110035
and printed by Pauls Press, New Delhi 110020
Binding by Saku

Dedicated with a prayer to the memory of
Sekar Asir Johnsingh; Pilot Officer Anup Singh Negi;
Major Sameer Katwal; numerous brave MIG 21 pilots
who flew into death, and thousands of security personnel
who have sacrificed their lives for the honour of the nation.

Contents

 Foreword

Going for a walk in an Indian forest with Dr A. J. T. Johnsingh is simply one of the finest experiences you can have in life. There is his good humor. There is the joy in his steps when he is walking in the forest. He walks to live, and lives to walk—and it shows. His good feelings set the whole tone of the trip. And you feel good because he is so at home in the forest. He is ever alert; completely aware of all that is going on around him. After you have walked with him for a while, you come to understand how he is thinking way in advance of where you are right now. He is timing his pace to avoid potential conflict, say with a bull elephant coming to drink in a forest pool. Or he is planning the path and pace of the walk to encounter and engage other species he has his mind set on seeing that day.

Dr Johnsingh is legendary for his ability to find and see wildlife. Nothing goes unnoticed. He names all the birds flitting about. He rattles off plant names. He identifies all animal tracks. Being the teacher that he is, Dr Johnsingh will question you about what he has told you earlier. He asks you to identify a bird the next time it is encountered, or questions you about streamside pugmarks and animal signs. The good-natured questioning comes from the master naturalist. It comes with deep feeling from a man who really cares about the wildlife and plant diversity that is India. Dr Johnsingh just wants to make it available to you, and to everyone. It is his passion. It is his life-work to really enjoy nature and to make it accessible to all of us. And if you are impressed with his enthusiasm on a walk in the forest, just wait until you go looking for mahseer with him!

We are very fortunate that Dr Johnsingh has taken the time to write down his stories from walks in the forest and mahseer-seeking trips. One great value of these stories is that, by recording his experiences and observations, he gives us a sense of the ecological change that is occurring in Indian forests and waterways. Retracing Jim Corbett's tracks is a good example. As a boy, Dr Johnsingh learned natural history from Jim Corbett's books. As a trained ecologist, he has gone back to those forests and walked those same trails to see how it is now. He reports this to us. In the future, other naturalists will walk the trails that Dr Johnsingh has walked, visit the places he has visited, and record the changes that have occurred in the time that has elapsed.

One of our biggest barriers in thinking about and understanding the manifestations of ecological change and imparting concern about change to a wide audience is what environmental historians call our collective ecological amnesia. A father can tell his son how it was, but the son, who has never experienced what his father has seen, simply cannot appreciate the changes in nature that are happening everywhere. For this reason, our collective idea of what is natural changes, usually for the worse. Ecologists recognize this and have given it a name: the shifting baseline. Consequently, our environmental history is not grounded and we simply do not see or understand the deterioration that is occurring.

But Dr Johnsingh is not pessimistic. He sees a growing conservation awareness in India's young people. He has spent his life imparting his enthusiasm to his many students at the Wildlife Institute of India. Now, through his stories, we can all begin to experience Dr Johnsingh's passion and his joy in experiencing nature and being the master naturalist that he is.

John Seidensticker, Ph.D.
Senior Scientist
Smithsonian National Zoological Park, Washington D.C.

 Preface and Acknowledgements

Jim Corbett is like a demi-God in my childhood memories. His absorbing descriptions of jungle lore kindled my desire to become a student of nature for life. Looking back, I am even indebted to Jim Corbett for rousing my desire to write of my experiences in the wilderness. Over the years, I published many of my articles in newspapers, books and wildlife magazines. I am grateful to these publications for permission to reproduce the following articles. I thank Dr Mahesh Rangarajan for prompting me to compile my articles in the form of a book.

Earlier versions of these articles or parts of them were published as below:

'On Jim Corbett's Trail': *Wildlife Institute of India (WII) Newsletter, Special Issue on Himalaya* (April–June 1994): 16–20; and *Blackbuck* (Vol. 10, 1994): 32–41 with G.S. Rawat, Wildlife Institute of India, Dehra Dun as co-author.

'The Whistling Hunter': Paola Manfredi (ed.), *In Danger* (Delhi: Ranthambhore Foundation, 1997): 90–5.

'The Tahr Hills': *WII Newsletter* (May–June 1990): 30–3 and *The Hindu* (1 September 1991).

'The Leap of the Goat Antelope': *Frontline* (June 1989): 82–5; *Sanctuary, Wildlife Institute Special* (1992): 32–5; *Hornbill* (October–December 1992): 28–32 and *Hornbill* (October–December 2001): 22–9.

'Mammoths at Love and War': *WII Newsletter* (July–September 1996): 7–11; and in *Sanctuary* (June 2002): 28–45 with Christy A. Williams, Areas Coordinator, WWF International as co-author.

'The Flight of the Mahseer': *Indian Society for Conservation Biology Newsletter* (January 1996–98): 4–7 with V.P. Ajith and Manoj Nair as co-authors; *The Hindu* (19 October 1997) and *Hornbill* (January–March, 2000): 24–7 with A.S. Negi, Indian Forest Service, Chief Wildlife Warden, Uttaranchal as co-author.

'Tracking the Lions of Gir': *The Hindu* (29 September, 1996) and *Hornbill* (July–September 1996): 2–7.

P.C. Tyagi, Ajay Desai, Justus Joshua, A. Udhayan, Ravi Chellam, Jamal A. Khan, Dhananjai Mohan, K. Sankar, Sathyakumar, Nima Manjrekar, Shomita Mukherjee, Ashraf, N.V.K., Vasant Saberwal, Nitin D. Rai, Prachi Mehta, Charudutt Mishra, Aparajita Datta, Christy A. Williams,

Manoj Nair, Yoganand, Rohan Arthur, Madhusudan, Kavitha Iswaran, Shankar Raman and Divya Mudappa were some of my numerous admirable students who have helped me both directly and indirectly in bringing out this book. Nima was of immense help in meticulously reading through almost all my writings. M.P. Aggarwal, my personal assistant, word-processed all my articles.

My wife Kousalya has stood steadfast behind me with her silent prayers. It is immensely satisfying to see my elder son Mike, a fighter pilot in the Indian Air Force, avidly taking to angling, trekking and wildlife photography. I am confident that soon the love for outdoor life will infect my younger son Mervin, who is in the process of becoming an electronics and communications engineer, enabling him to enjoy the thrills of the wilderness.

I have also been struck by the pangs of tragedy. Jothi, who accompanied me to the tahr hills, died at the ripe age of eighty-five, while Sekar, one of my younger brothers, who also accompanied me there, succumbed to a tetanus infection when he was just twenty-six. This untimely death of my brother, who was stepping into the shoes of my father as a Physical Education teacher, devastated my father who, I would say, was afraid neither of man nor of beast. I have gone through the terrifying experience of witnessing the killing of Mr N.R. Nair, a fine officer from the Indian Forest Service, by a young tusker in the Bandipur Tiger Reserve.

My observations over the last thirty years in different parts of the country force me to conclude that we are in the process of losing our valuable and fascinating wildlife in pockets of wildlife habitats. Nevertheless, the growing spirit of conservation in the country give us the flicker of hope, that in spite of increasing problems, the nimble-footed tahr and goral, enigmatic dhole, awe-inspiring tiger, majestic elephant, lion, and the mighty mahseer, are going to be around to delight our children's children for generations to come.

A. J. T. Johnsingh
Dehradun
October 2003

1 🌳 In the Beginning

I now live in the foothills of the northernmost mountain ranges of India, but my life began in the southern end of south India, in Sankar Nagar, a housing 'colony'. Nanguneri was a small town near Sankar Nagar, and it was there, one dusty afternoon, that I accidentally discovered a Tamil translation of Jim Corbett's *Maneaters of Kumaon*. I came upon the book on the wrong shelf in a corner of the library. As I greedily turned its pages it cast a spell on me that still has not lifted.

I would say that I was 'pre-adapted' for a career in wildlife. My father, Joseph Asirvatham, was a Physical Education Teacher in the nearby school, Sankar Reddiar Board High School. He had represented the volleyball team of Madras State—then undivided—for seven consecutive years. He was an excellent coach under whom the school had produced champion athletes. He preferred the outdoor life to any other.

For many years, my mother, Mercy, also taught in the same school. She grew a lot of plants and kept unusual pets: she had a three-striped palm squirrel and a Red-vented bulbul. She, with her five brothers, grew up in Kerala, in the Tenmalai-Achankoil area, where my grandfather worked in British times, clearing virgin forest for tea and rubber.

Nanguneri is situated in the rain-shadow area of the southern Western Ghats, and as a result, the tract around is semi-arid, with plant species such as *Acacia planifrons, Borassus flabellifer, Euphorbia antiquorum* and the exotic *Prosopis juliflora.* The nearby stream, which comes from the Kalakad hills, remains dry for most parts of the year, with a beach-like sandy riverbed. Yet, there is grey partridge, hedgehog, black-naped hare, Indian fox, common mongoose and jungle cat. Jackals were rare. The Tamil Nadu Forest Department, as was the tradition in most parts of the country, issued small game licences for an annual fee of Rs. 30. Small game hunting with catapult and gun, with our country-bred hound-like dogs, Johnny and Jilly, was one of our favourite pastimes.

In those days, the rains were prompt and bounteous, and the tanks around our home were perennial, with lots of fish. With my brothers Sunder and Sekar, I swam in these tanks and agricultural wells, and fished with simple hooks, fishing lines and bamboo rods with earthworm as bait. At the height of the northeast monsoon, which came right through October, November and December, abundant waterfowl, particularly teals and pintail ducks, thronged the tanks, providing another excellent and challenging opportunity for hunting. We shot them when they were on the water's edge, and this often involved crawling for several tens of metres, using clumps of bushes as cover, to reach within the range of the single-barrel shotgun that my father possessed. We often used reloaded cartridges. All three of us were very good at fishing and hunting.

What gave us ample exercise and excitement was hunting grey partridge. If anyone wanted to shoot grey partridge around Nanguneri, he had to be fleet-footed and have very good eyesight. We hunted the partridges either in the morning or in the evening, and it required a lot of skill. First of all, the birds needed to be located, a difficult task, as the birds, at least around Nanguneri, had the habit of skulking to cover on seeing people even at distances of 500 metres. Then the partridges had to be cornered, for shooting them with reloaded cartridges from the shotgun could only be done from a short distance. This often involved a lot of absurd running alongside the bird to chase it to a convenient corner, taking care not to run behind it, so it was not frightened into flying off as far as it was capable. In the early years of our hunting, we shot partridges throughout the year. Later, we came across literature that championed the ethics of hunting, saying birds should not be hunted during the breeding season; after this we refrained from shooting for four or five months from February onwards.

One annual event which our family and friends anxiously

looked forward to, was the three- to five-day camp in the foothills of the Thirukkurungudi range, in what is now the Kalakad-Mundanthurai Tiger Reserve. Our usual destination was the guard quarters—now in ruins—built by the British on the left bank of the Nambiar river, very close to the forest boundary. My mother and two sisters happily joined us on this outing. The local Range Forest Officer was informed about our trip and then we'd set off. Sometimes my mother and sisters would go by bus and then by bullock cart to the camp, while we, the 'men', walked the twenty kilometres from Sankar Nagar to the camp, taking a short cut across the countryside. We would spend the days exploring the jungle and fishing in the river. Occasionally, a hare, a mouse deer or a grey junglefowl, which were plentiful in those days even in the forest boundary, was shot for the pot.

After reading *Maneaters of Kumaon*, our trips to the jungle became even more exciting. We imagined maneating tigers all around our camp, behind every rock and bush. At night we'd whisper our conversations, for fear of attracting maneating tigers. Once our dog Johnny accompanied us to the jungle, and the night we reached the camp, I saw my first leopard, hardly three metres from the path along which we were walking. In the torchlight, the leopard rose, fully visible from nose tip to tail end, glowing whitish yellow amidst the green bushes and black rocks. As we retreated, it quietly crawled back into cover.

The next morning, my father took me, fourteen years old then, for my first hunt in the jungle. The fear that the leopard might harm Johnny made us leave him behind in camp. We walked for about two kilometres from the camp, and came to a medium sized patch of scrub jungle. Here my father loaded the gun with one reloaded cartridge filled with shots, gave me the gun and one more reloaded cartridge. He placed me at the eastern end of the scrub, and went to the other end to flush grey junglefowl towards me. Before leaving he said that I should shoot the bird only when I was sure to kill it.

As his footsteps crunched away, I felt alone and afraid. What if a leopard or a sloth bear or a big boar, rather than junglefowl, came rushing towards me and my inadequate weapon? Nevertheless, I sat motionless in my 'hide' between two rocks amidst bushes. After many, many, very, very long minutes, I heard the distant clapping of my father, and as I regained my courage and strength, two junglefowl, a cock in its beautiful breeding plumage, and a hen, rushed towards me. They probably saw me, because when I raised my gun, they both stopped dead at a distance of about ten metres. I took quick aim and fired, felling both the birds.

I left the gun on the forest floor, to run and pick up the birds. Suddenly, Johnny appeared seemingly from nowhere, leaped in the air, and grabbed one of the birds from my hand. He placed it on the ground, and whining, whimpering and furiously wagging his tail, he circled me and my father, who

had by this time joined us. Johnny had 'escaped' from the camp compound and tracked us through the jungle. It was a very happy trio that returned to the camp.

I went to St. Xavier's College in Palayankottai, then called the 'Oxford of south India', for my pre-University course and undergraduate degree in Zoology. During my four years in the college, I read almost all of Jim Corbett. I felt fascinated by the animals that cropped up in his tales, particularly the mahseer, goral, sambar, kakar or barking deer, leopard and tiger. I longed to catch a mahseer and see the areas described by Jim Corbett.

I vividly remember many of my professors. M. V. Rajendran, our Zoology Professor, an expert on snakes, fondly called 'Snake-teacher', got me even more interested in animals than I was. Prof. J. X. Arachi cultivated in me an interest in plants. Prof. R. Ponnarasu, our Tamil teacher, extolled the virtues of exercises, games and a disciplined life. He was a model for the students with his excellent tennis and ball badminton.

Once out of B.Sc. in 1965, I wanted a job either in the Army or with the Forest Department. I didn't think I would be at university, but my destiny, or God, had other plans for me. When I opened the newspaper for the examination results, I was amazed to see I was second in Madras University. I decided to apply for a seat in M.Sc. Zoology in Madras Christian College. Soon after the M. Sc., I got a job as a lecturer in Zoology in Ayya Nadar Janaki Ammal College, a new institution in

Sivakasi, a grubby town famous for lithoworks, matchboxes and firecrackers. There, with my students, and two colleagues in the Zoology Department, Murali and Paramanandham (Params), I went many times to the nearby Rajapalayam and Srivilliputtur hills. We studied peafowl around Sivakasi, and whenever I went to Nanguneri, I observed the Indian fox. I published my first article, for which I was paid twelve rupees, in *The Indian Express* in 1972, about a bird sanctuary near Tirunelveli. Two of my colleagues and friends, Nainan Samuel and P.K.Sasidharan, both in the English Department, were of immense help in my early days of writing.

One turning point in my life was my meeting in the Kalakad hills in May 1971 with Mr J.C. Daniel, Director, Bombay Natural History Society (BNHS), who turned me towards wildlife studies. My meeting with Mr Daniel initially led me to a preliminary study on dholes in the Masinagudi area near Mudumalai Wildlife Sanctuary, under the guidance of Dr Michael Fox, an expert from the USA on dogs and other canids. The study was done for a total period of five months in 1973 and 1975. 'Cheetal Walk', the jungle home of E.R.C. Davidar, was our base. Davidar was a lawyer by profession, but a good wildlife photographer, naturalist and conservationist who wrote a vivid account of his wilderness experiences in *Cheetal Walk* (Delhi, 1996). The dhole study taught me to walk alone in the elephant country, and eventually led to my doing a study on dholes in the Bandipur Tiger Reserve in Karnataka from August 1976 to July 1978 for my Ph.D. Before leaving for Bandipur, in May 1976, I surveyed the southern Western Ghats for Nilgiri tahr, in collaboration with Mr Davidar; the article in this book on the Nilgiri tahr explains part of my survey.

I spent almost two years in Bandipur walking through the forest studying the dhole. It was the most remarkable period in my life. I emerged from there exultant to be whole and alive, despite many months in an area with more elephants than anywhere else in Asia. It was a wonderful area for the elephant, but perhaps a little less so for a lone human walking about. I came out with numerous itching tick bites and lots of information on the hitherto little-known dhole. There was no guidance from anyone, except George B. Schaller in the form of his pioneering book, *The Deer and the Tiger*, which was my guru.

One remarkable person I met during my dhole study was Valerius Geist, an authority on wild ungulates, from the University of Calgary, Canada. He did a remarkable study of bighorn sheep in the Canadian Rocky Mountains, habituating them to his presence by giving them salt. Geist, in fact, came to Bandipur to help one of Madhav Gadgil's students (of the Indian Institute of Science, Bangalore), and in him I found a passionate wildlifer. 'Johnsingh,' he would often say, 'let us freeze among the rocks and watch animals.'

Dr Gadgil had been convinced that the dhole is one species

in the Indian jungles that cannot be studied. At the end of my study he offered me a fellowship to write my thesis at the Centre for Theoretical Studies (CTS), Indian Institute of Science. Fortunately for me, in my early days at CTS, I met J.F. Eisenberg and Devra Kleiman from the Smithsonian Institution, Washington DC. I went with them to Bandipur and Mudumalai for a few days. They were impressed by my field skills, but realised that I needed more training to evolve into a better wildlife biologist. They left me in Bangalore with the assurance that at an appropriate time I would be awarded a fellowship to spend some time with other biologists at the Smithsonian Institution.

After submitting my thesis in June 1979, I went back to the Sivakasi College for a year, when I did a study on white-headed babblers with Params. The promised fellowship offer from Dr Eisenberg came in March 1980, and in May, with my wife Kousalya and son Mike Johnsingh, I was in the Conservation and Research Center (CRC) at Front Royal, a facility owned and managed by the Smithsonian Institution.

My guru at Front Royal was John Seidensticker, who studied tigers and leopard in Asia. My task at CRC was to capture, radio-collar and radio-track small carnivores. The small carnivore assemblage at the CRC, which had grasslands and broad-leaved forests, included raccoon, opossum, red fox, bobcat and skunk. In spite of my experience in field research, I found I had a lot of wildlife techniques to learn. John remains one of my mentors.

His plate is full, looking after the mammals of the National Zoo, Smithsonian Institution, and working to save wild tigers and the giant panda, but he readily agreed to write the foreword to this book when I requested him.

Towards the end of June 1980, Devra and John took me to Dillon, Montana. There were many firsts during this trip. At John's family ranch around Twin Bridges, I walked in my first snow, and saw my first pronghorn antelope. Then we drove to Yellowstone, the world's first National Park, where in the company of Richard Knight, who was studying bears, we caught and radio-collared a black bear. For the first time, I flew a CESSNA 210 aircraft and radio-tracked black bears and grizzlies.

At this time I finally met George B. Schaller, who, unknown to himself, had guided me through his book all those years ago. He is an eminent wildlife biologist, who has studied numerous charismatic species such as the mountain gorilla, African lion, tiger, jaguar, snow leopard and giant panda. He is a hero to all young wildlife biologists the world over. He came to the Smithsonian Institution to give a talk on the giant panda, which he was then studying in China. Eisenberg, who was one of my thesis examiners and the world's leading mammalogist, had sent him a copy of my thesis. During the brief meeting I had with him, Schaller alerted me to the danger of falling into a rut when I returned to India: don't end up in a university teaching ninety per cent of your time, he had cautioned. He said that I should continue my field research. I have tried to live up to his advice.

When I was back in India to make a living, Mr Daniel came to my help again. He gave me a job as Project Scientist on the BNHS Elephant Project. He sent me to Arunachal Pradesh to see its elephant habitat, and to Dehra Dun to explore the possibility of joining the upcoming Wildlife Institute of India (WII). My job with BNHS was very useful, as it gave me the opportunity to visit the Corbett Tiger Reserve, Arunachal Pradesh, and different wildlife habitats in the Western Ghats south of Coorg.

In early January 1985, I was offered the job of Deputy Director, WII, which I immediately accepted. It has been a wonderful opportunity. I have worked with many wildlife species, and visited different wildlife habitats in the country and abroad. I have learned a lot from Alan Rodgers and John Sale, experts hired by the Government of India to help establish the Institute. The Institute, then administered by H.S. Panwar, its first director, provided an excellent atmosphere for wildlife research and conservation.

Beginning as a self-taught naturalist, I have evolved into a professional wildlife biologist. What I present in this book is based on almost thirty years of experience in wildlife and conservation in various places in the country and abroad. During these long years of field research, with a silent prayer in my heart, I have walked hundreds of kilometres through dense bush and tall grass, ideal resting places for all forms of potentially dangerous animals. It hasn't all been without excitement. On unnerving occasions I have been chased by an elephant or charged by a tigress or king cobra. I attribute my safety to the prayers of my family. We believe in Psalm 91: 'for He shall give His angels charge over thee.... thou shalt tread upon the lion and adder ... I will be with him in trouble ... I will deliver him and honour him.'

2   On Jim Corbett's Trail

Returning to the Temple Tiger

Reading *The Temple Tiger* by Jim Corbett, no one can miss his absorbing description of a patch of dense jungle about three kilometres south of Devidhura in the Kumaon Himalaya. Early in the twentieth century, when Corbett pursued the 'temple' tiger of Devidhura, this jungle had sambar, barking deer, langur and numerous pheasants. Corbett vividly describes a fight between a black bear and tiger in a ravine late one evening, that he heard as he perched on a branch two metres above the ground, waiting for the temple tiger to appear. As the bear and tiger fought in a small hollow, the sounds of the fight were terrifying; he was thankful that the fight was between two contestants capable of defending themselves and not a three-cornered one in which he was involved. He missed the tiger because of 'rank bad shooting' and shot dead the bear as it screamed and rushed towards him.

In late April 1993, eighty-four years after Corbett's visit, I was exploring the same forest. I was with my colleague, Dr G.S. Rawat, a man from the Kumaon Himalaya. Since our boyhood, when we read Corbett's books, we had wanted to return to some of the places where Corbett had hunted. We decided to see the areas between Kaladhungi and Tanakpur, where Corbett had shot the Mukteshwar, Champawat, Chuka and Thak maneaters. The distance from Kaladhungi to Tanakpur via Mukteshwar, Champawat and Chuka, is 300 kilometres. We planned a ten-day trip in late April 1993, and since time was a constraint, we used a jeep.

Naturally, change was in evidence everywhere. The dense oak and scrub jungle near Devidhura that Corbett mentions, has been lost to cultivation. In place of the single grass hut village, there were numerous masonry houses. It was a cloudy day punctuated with distant thunder and our walk up the ridge, still densely forested, was an enjoyable one. We walked for two hours as silently as possible, looking for pheasants and large mammals. The cooing of the Rufous Turtle Dove, calls of the Great Hill Barbet and songs of cowherd boys rang through the forest. Red-billed Blue Magpies flew through the forest canopy and across the valleys. A group of White-throated Laughing Thrushes rummaged through the understorey in a dense patch of oak and rhododendron. There were a few wild pig diggings and a patch of barking deer pellets. There was no evidence of either black bear or sambar. It was apparent that the jungle had ceased to be a habitat for the tiger a long time ago.

Between 1907 and 1938, Jim Corbett, the legendary hunter and renowned story teller, had shot eight maneating tigers and two maneating leopards in the Kumaon hills. These maneaters had killed about nine hundred people. Much has changed in these hills since then, as in many other parts of the world. The bridle paths, where men and their horses walked for days to reach a destination, have been converted into motorable roads where buses roar past each other now. Pati (a village Corbett calls Pali in his account of the Champawat maneater) with a population of about fifty people in 1907, now has about 2500 people. The major victims of this change are the forests and wildlife.

Mukteshwar

Rhododendron was in bloom when we went to Mukteshwar. Its scarlet flowers stood out among the white, light green and rusty new foliage of three species of oak. Corbett had shot the Mukteshwar tigress near an orchard owned by his friend Badri Shah. Luckily, we met Ramesh Lal Shah, Badri's nephew, who has been looking after the orchard since Badri's death in 1925. Ramesh remembered glimpsing Corbett as a boy. He showed us the ravine where Corbett had shot the Mukteshwar tigress. Now farmland and houses on either side of the ravine has edged out the forest, which is scanty. Shah briefed us about the decline of wildlife in and around Mukteshwar. He had last seen a tiger on his farm about six years before our visit. Sambar has become almost extinct, although it still occurs in the 13 kms² well-protected jungle around the hundred-year-old Indian Veterinary Research Institute and in the Ramgarh hills, 16 kilometres south of Mukteshwar as the crow flies. These hills, which we saw on our way to Mukteshwar, were well wooded even during our survey. Tigers were reported to stray from the foothills and in certain pockets, nature still dominated. However, in Kasyalekh, five kilometres north of the Ramgarh forests, it had been forty years since the last tiger was shot or seen in the vicinity of the village. We saw the pitiful remains of the tiger in the house of a villager: a head with broken teeth, the mouth painted red.

Champawat

In Corbett's time, a tigress known as the Champawat maneater arrived in Kumaon as a full-fledged maneater from Nepal. She was driven out of Nepal by a body of armed Nepalese after she had killed two hundred people, and during the four years that she had been in Kumaon, she had added 244 to her tally of victims. Corbett was asked by the government to track down this maneater. He began looking for this tigress in 1907, after she killed a woman in Pati who was cutting leaf-fodder with a few other women. When Corbett reached Pati from Nainital

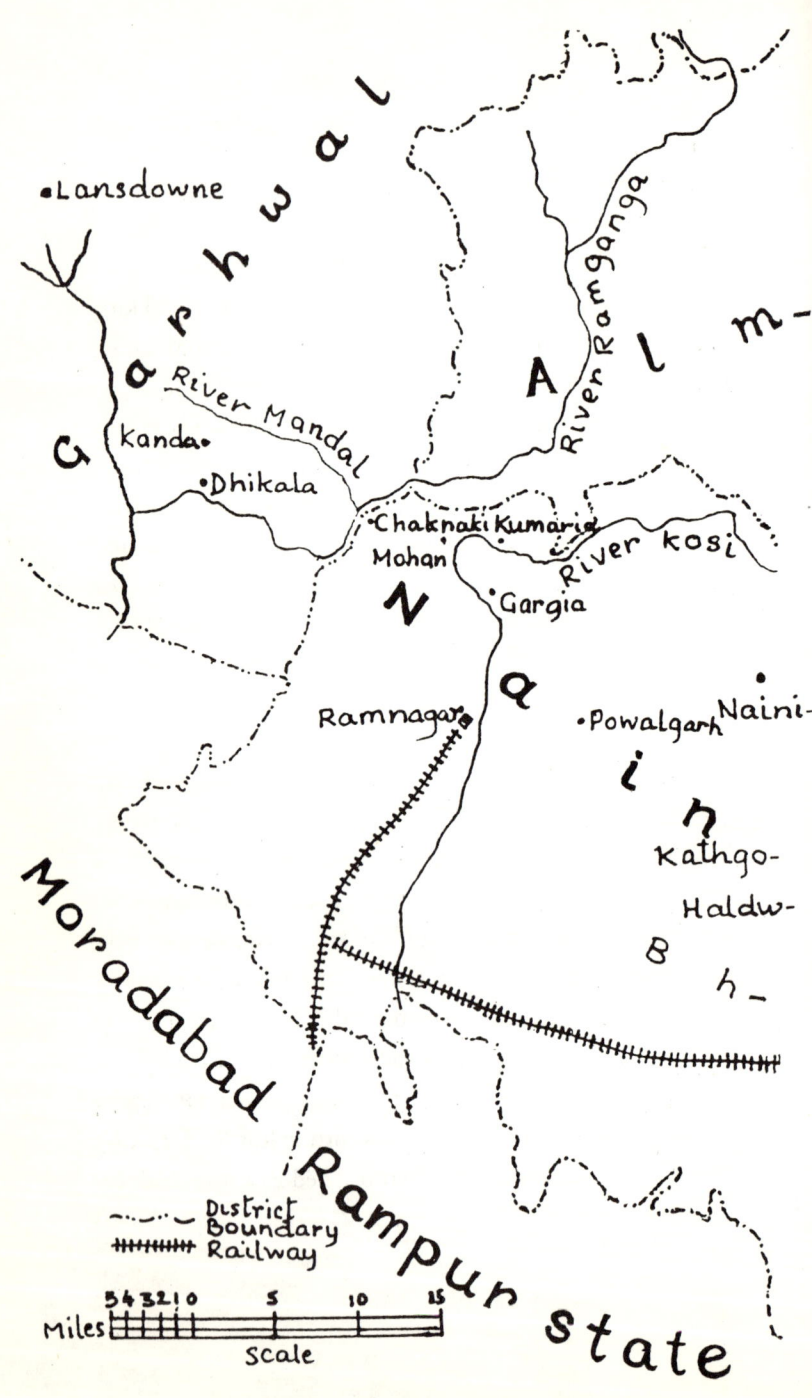

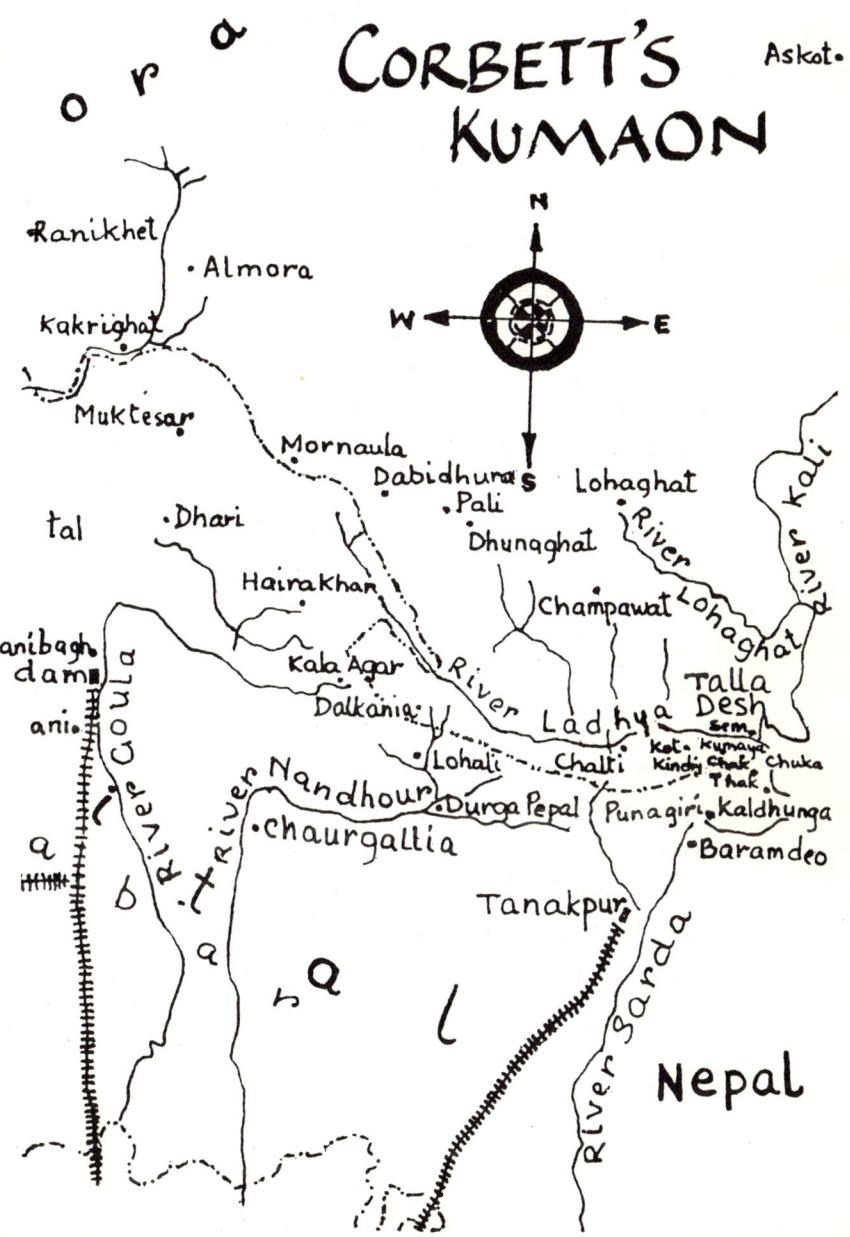

after three days of walking and travelling by pony, it had been five days since the woman had been killed. During those five days, the villagers said, no one had gone beyond their own doorsteps; Corbett observes in his book that the insanitary conditions of the courtyard testified to the truth of their statement.

Corbett saw the densely wooded ravine where the woman was killed. As night approached, he seemed to court death sitting on the road to wait for the tigress, which was reported to be wandering around the village. He was only thirty-three years old then and inexperienced at hunting maneating tigers. Through the miserably cold, long night, he was frightened by visions of a dozen tigers advancing on him. Fortunately for him, the tiger was nowhere in the vicinity of the village. When his men found him early the next morning, he was fast asleep, his head resting on his drawn-up knees. Corbett could not kill the Champawat maneater near Pati, but before he left the village, he shot three goral in one of the grass-covered steep ridges nearby. His men ate one, and the villagers shared the other two.

After exploring the forest south of Devidhura, we set out towards Pati. The striking feature of the habitat close to Pati was the rolling hills interspersed with steep ridges, covered with grass and pine, even now ideal goral habitat. Like Devidhura village and its temple, which have changed because of human population growth and modernisation, Pati also sprang a surprise on us. Along the deserted road where Corbett had waited alone for the maneater through one terrifying night, there were numerous teashops. Instead of a few grass-thatched huts, was a prosperous village of more than a hundred concrete houses. Several villagers, however, remembered the stories related to the death of the woman and Corbett's visit. With the help of the villagers, we even tracked down the great grandson of the woman killed by the maneater. The village headman, seventy-two years old, a descendant of the headman during Corbett's days, took us to the place where the maneater had killed the woman. Corbett describes a ravine, but there wasn't one. Instead there was a broad valley devoid of vegetation. Hardly fifty metres from the place where the woman was killed, there was a noisy school with at least fifty children between six and ten years of age.

Every villager we interviewed said that tiger and sambar no longer occured on these hills, but goral and barking deer were still common. We had doubts even about this reported wildlife abundance, as the area showed signs of excessive use by cattle and people and numerous trails criss-crossed the hills. Three kilometres east of the village was a ridge covered with dense forest that looked to us as though it might still hold some wildlife. One villager remarked that the ridge was one place where sambar and black bear could still be sighted.

The pleasant cloudy weather we had the day before had changed. It was warm and sultry. We climbed the ridge and wandered about for an hour, looking for animals. We saw signs neither of goral nor of barking deer. We saw the ill-conceived, abortive attempt of the Forest Department to raise deodar trees amidst the dense pine, oak and rhododendron forest. Many rhododendron trees had been felled for firewood. While descending to the road, we met a man who was nervously herding away his goats from the ridge. He said leopards were still numerous, they killed many sheep and goat, and were responsible for the decline of the goral population. At night, we halted in the Dhunaghat forest rest house tucked away amidst pine trees.

Everyone we talked to about wildlife around Champawat, told us about the forest patch between Khetikhan (five kilometres from Dhunaghat) and Champawat. If you follow the road the distance between Khetikhan and Champawat is 33 kilometres. We decided to walk the fifteen-kilometre short cut through the forest and over two hills. We left Khetikhan around 7 a.m. and walked at an easy pace, looking for birds and signs of large mammals. When we were about five kilometres from Champawat, we recalled an incident Corbett narrates, which had occurred almost in the same area.

Corbett's story goes thus. Twenty men were walking along this forest road, and about midday, they were startled by the agonised cries of a human being from the valley below. They cowered in fright at the edge of the road as the cries drew nearer and nearer, and into view came a tiger carrying a naked woman. The woman's hair was trailing on the ground on one side of the tiger and her feet trailed on the other. The tiger was holding her by the small of her back, and she was beating her chest and calling alternately to God and man for help. The tiger passed with its burden a mere fifty metres from the men, clearly visible to them. When the cries had faded into the distance, the men continued on their way. When Corbett asked them later why they did nothing, the men replied that they were afraid, and asked, what can men do when they are frightened?

On the outskirts of Champawat, off the Pithoragarh road, was a narrow road which had a signboard with a picture of a tiger and information that the 'Champawat maneater' was shot three kilometres from there. We walked along the road, and eventually realised that the distance was probably closer to three miles. A few boys we met on the path took us to the particular point at the gorge where the maneater had been shot eighty-four years before. The area was the most beautiful we had seen during the trip. The Gaida river flowed through the deep gorge, forming pools of blue water. The hills around the gorge rose sharply for 300–400 metres. On the steep slopes stood columns of pine trees, and many rhododendrons in bloom. Except for an abandoned road, built about twenty years earlier on the left bank of the gorge, to a small hydro-electric powerhouse (which was not functional) the area looked undisturbed. The serenity in the gathering darkness was so infectious in that wild setting, we thought we would hear a tiger calling any time.

Thak and Chuka

From Champawat, our next destination was Chuka in Ladiya valley. The drive to Chalti, forty kilometres from Champawat, took us for the first ten kilometres through excellent oak-rhododendron forests, and thereafter there were patches of cultivation. Coming down to an altitude of a thousand metres, the vegetation changed drastically. Sal trees with golden yellow leaves dominated, and the Indian Coral tree (*Erythrina indica*) with its coral red flowers, replaced rhododendron.

We started walking at nine a.m. from Chalti towards Chuka along the Ladiya valley. Even so early in the day, the temperature soared above 35°C. The hills on either side rose steeply for 300–500 m; according to our local guide, there was an abundance of goral and an occasional serow in that area. In several places, we had to cross the meandering Ladiya River, and therefore the going was slow. The human population in the valley was sparse and distributed in five villages ranging in size from two to ten houses. There were quite a few sambar tracks in the riverbed. People were collecting dead and fallen logs, and there were three water-powered mills for making wooden vessels. The mill owners who were making many more vessels than their permitted quota, complained that the tree species Sanan (*Ougeinia oojeinensis*) and Genthi (*Boehmeria rugulosa*), suitable for making vessels, were—for reasons inexplicable to them—becoming rarer and rarer in the valley!

In 1937, a tiger known as the Chuka maneater, and in 1938, a tigress known as the Thak maneater, caused terror in the valley: the latter, in fact, almost bringing to a halt the work of about five thousand labourers extracting timber from the Ladiya valley. Even now, Thak and Chuka can only be reached on foot, either from Chalti or Thuligad. Fifty years ago, access to these areas was even more difficult, and how the sixty-four year old Corbett reached these places within a short span of time, and how he outwitted these tigers, can be fully appreciated only by those who have seen the terrain.

We reached Chuka in the evening, and went to the Ladiya–Sharda confluence to try and catch mahseer. Corbett talks of splendid fishing at this junction. Although we tried hard for two hours, we did not have a single bite. The evening, however, was not dull. The rolling of rocks on the slopes across the river in Nepal alerted us. We scanned the slopes with binoculars, and were rewarded by the sight of five goral coming down to drink water.

When we left for Chuka that morning, we had no idea what the village was like, and had thought that we would be able to buy some food there. Chuka's human population, we found, had declined over the last fifty years. It had a few houses, but we realised soon enough that it would not be possible to buy any food. However, sixty-two year old Ummed Singh, the headman of Chuka, who had seen Corbett as a boy, bailed us out with the usual large-heartedness of hill people. We were hungry and tired after our long day in the hot sun. He gave us dinner of dried goat curry and *roti*, and a place to sleep on his terrace. The cloudless sky was studded with stars and the Sharda River roared nearby. No alarm calls came from the jungle. Only the barking of the dogs broke the silence of the night. We slept soundly.

Next morning, we left for Thak. The distance was about four kilometres, but the walk involved a steep climb through dense sal forest. On the way, Ummed Singh showed us the rock on which Corbett lay down, and mimicking the call of the maneater which was looking for a mate, lured it closer and shot it dead. Near Thak, which still matched Corbett's description, we saw the giant mango tree, from the roots of which issues a cold spring of clear water. Both the Thak maneater and Corbett had drunk from this spring. We also quenched our thirst here, after the steep climb in the hot April sun.

Kaladhunga

If the climb to Thak, which is atop a hillock, was very steep, the descent to Kaladhunga forest bungalow, our next destination, was even steeper. Ummed Singh, after showing us the way to Kaladhunga from the top of the Thak hillock, bid us farewell. We reached Kaladhunga an hour later. When Corbett visited Kaladhunga in 1938, there was no human habitation as far as he could see, and judging from the tiger and other animal calls that he heard from the bungalow, he concluded that the area was extremely rich in game. We found the forest bungalow unused except by some shepherds. The view of the Sharda in front of the bungalow was blocked by overgrown vegetation. Vandalism, possibly by poachers from Nepal, had destroyed the wire mesh and glass panes of the windows at the bungalow. As darkness gathered, we pulled two wooden cots out onto the verandah and settled for the night. There were no alarm calls that night, and it seemed like all wildlife had deserted the area.

Next morning, in order to avoid the heat of the day, we left Kaladhunga when there was just enough light to walk by. Along the path, we went past the Purnagiri temple, which runs parallel to the Sharda gorge. The gorge reminded me of the time Corbett saw some mysterious lights in the hills across the Sharda River, when he was camping near the river on his way to the territory of the Tallades maneater. We completed the fourteen-kilometre walk to Thuligad at 8.30 in the morning. Our driver was waiting here for us. The drive back to Dehradun took the rest of the day.

As boys, when we read Corbett's stories, we had visions of the hills around Pati with plentiful goral, the forests around Devidhura populated by sambar with antlers as big as the branch of an oak tree, and the Sharda full of big mahseer. The years have changed this wildlife abundance. Instead, everywhere, we saw evidence only of human abundance. On the bank of the Sharda opposite Kaladhunga, where sambar and barking deer flitted through the forest fifty years ago, there is now a village called Sananni, with about three hundred houses. The Nepalese have not only shot out the wildlife on their land, they frequently cross the Sharda on inflated rubber tubes, and decimate wildlife on the Indian side. Numerous Indian poachers also contribute to eradicating fish and wildlife. Ummed Singh claims that ten years ago he had counted twelve barking deer on a walk between Chuka and Kaladhunga. Now he hardly sees any.

Nevertheless, wildlife conservation in Corbett's Kumaon could be strengthened by the creation of a Sharda Biosphere Reserve, covering an area of about 2000 kms². If Nepal also contributed to this conservation effort by creating a similar Biosphere Reserve on the other side of the Sharda River, various forms of Outer Himalayan wildlife could be protected in an area of about 4000 kms². Poaching needs to be controlled immediately. Special efforts need to be made to confiscate all illegal guns. Legal gun owners should be advised not to poach wildlife. Destructive ways of fishing, with poison and dynamites, in the tributaries of the Sharda where the masheer go spawning, needs to be stopped. Fishing in the river, which was once home to the Gangetic dolphin, needs to be regulated. Existing patches of natural vegetation in the suggested biosphere area have to be assiduously protected, and eco-restoration programmes initiated in degraded areas. The suggested biosphere area may never again echo with tiger roars and sambar alarm calls. But barking deer and goral would reappear on the slopes, and leopards would again be an everyday sight. The Sharda would become the favoured home of the mighty mahseer once more.

3 The Whistling Hunter

It was early on a winter morning in 1977. From my room in Bandipur village, the shooting hide near Thavarakatte—the pond in the Bandipur Tiger Reserve—was a kilometre away. Thin mist made a Japanese water colour of the forests around the pond. I walked cautiously towards the hide, looking out for wild elephants.

The shooting hide, built long ago by a Mysore maharajah, was in the middle of dense *Lantana*, bamboo and dry deciduous forests which had an abundant population of wild pig, chital and sambar. Tiger, leopard and dhole naturally hunted in this area frequently. The hide had mud walls, with several holes to shoot through, and a tin roof. It stood under a large *Terminalia bellerica* tree. Visibility was much better from the shooting hide as a road ran in front of it for about 200 metres and a ten metre view-line cut through the scrub to the left of the hide for about 150 metres. I had discovered that Thavarakatte was

the best place in Bandipur to observe large mammals. I used to sit either inside, or on the rooftop or on a tree to wait for dholes. Exciting encounters with elephants were numerous in this area as well as tiger and leopard sightings.

Soon after I sat down on the hide's rooftop, a lone sambar's alarm call broke the silence of the forest. This was followed by many alarm calls of sambar and peafowl, a sign of the presence of a large predator. I stood on the rooftop for a minute, carefully looked on either side of the view-line to verify that there were no elephants and then jumped down from the rooftop and hurried to a large rosewood tree (*Dalbergia latifolia*) closer to the view-line, about 100 metres from the hide.

I often went to the forest in rubber *hawai chappals*: I found these best for wading through water, walking over mud and climbing trees. I had to climb trees several times in a week to avoid elephants and find a comfortable and safe perch to wait for and watch dholes. Wearing flip flops had a flip side though: it made me vulnerable to Russell's viper (*Vipera russelli*) and the common cobra (*Naja naja*) which I frequently encountered. But this vulnerability forced me to tread the jungle carefully and silently, which is vital in approaching and observing shy animals in a dense forest.

By the time I had perched on a large branch about four metres from the ground, the jungle around me was painted by the golden light of the morning sun. As I sat watching, with camera and binoculars on my lap, a sambar stag in magnificent hard antlers ran out from the scrub jungle in front of me. I could hear the commotion of several animals running through the scrub jungle.

Soon six dholes came trotting on the view-line from my left and when they came closer to my tree they stood, spread in a single line within a distance of fifteen or twenty metres, facing the scrub jungle. Their soft whines, restlessness and the occasional twitching of muscles on their bodies indicated that they were all excited by the impending morning hunt. I looked towards the area which the dholes were intently watching and soon discerned the movement of animals walking through the scrub jungle in the direction of my tree.

The first to emerge was an adult sambar doe. Meanwhile, the dholes had come closer, facing the trail along which the sambar was emerging. I was so tense with excitement I could barely breathe. The sambar doe emerged from the scrub with an extended neck and dilated nostrils. She had rolled back her eyeballs so that the whites of her eyes were visible. Every hair on her neck stood erect. She snorted and stamped her forefeet as she walked. It was a formidable threat display.

Contrary to my expectations, the dholes, instead of pouncing on the doe and tearing her to pieces, split into two groups, giving enough space for the doe to walk through safely. A yearling and another adult doe followed the first doe; all of them walked through the dholes unharmed. Meanwhile some more dholes, which had flushed out these sambars, joined the six on the view-line and entered the scrub jungle behind my tree. A little later a muffled scream of a fawn, which was immediately followed by the cracking of bones, indicated that the dholes had eaten their morning snack. After the hunt, the dholes probably went to the pond to drink because when I saw them again they were all coming from that direction. They lay down to rest when they came to the cool shade of a rosewood tree. A little later four sambar does came out of the scrub and, as a team, chased the dholes here and there. The dholes pranced about playfully with the sambar chasing them. I contemplated how inappropriate it is to call these graceful hunters 'bloody killers' as they normally are.

These Asiatic wild dogs are rust or sand coloured, weigh around 16 kilograms, and stand approximately 50 centimetres at the shoulder. Their length, including a long, black, bushy tail, is about 135 centimetres. Females are somewhat slighter of build but cannot easily be differentiated from males at a distance.

Of the dhole's nine sub-species, three definitely occur in India. These are *Cuon alpinus laniger* in Kashmir and Ladakh, *Cuon alpinus primaevus* in Garhwal, Kumaon, Nepal, Sikkim and Bhutan and *Cuon alpinus dukhunensis* south of the Ganges. The dholes found in the Namdapha area in Arunachal Pradesh could be *Cuon alpinus adjusts* from northern Burma. The genus *Cuon* is distinguished from *Canis* by the more rounded ears and proportionately short muzzle, a characteristic that gives dholes their extremely powerful bite. Dholes have only two molars on either side of the lower jaw instead of the usual three. Thus the dental formula for *Cuon* is incisors 3/3, canines 1/1, premolars 4/4, molars 2/2 = 40. The usual pattern in the family *Canidae* is incisors 3/3, canines 1/1, premolars 4/4 and molars 2/3 = 42.

Dholes used to occur as far north as the Altai Mountains of the former USSR, perhaps as far north as southern Siberia, where they are now extinct. From there their range extended radically southward encompassing Mongolia, much of China, Thailand, Indo-China, the Malaya Peninsula, Sumatra and Java. Dholes occur in Tibet, Nepal and India but not in Sri Lanka, Borneo and Japan.

They occupy an enormous variety of habitats. In the northern reaches of their range dholes inhabit dense forests, river gorges and mountainous alpine regions. In Ladakh and Tibet they inhabit cold wind-swept deserts. In the rest of India they exist almost exclusively in dense forests and thick scrub jungles where there is sufficient prey and water. Dense montane forests are their preferred habitat in Thailand.

Not long ago hunters and wildlife managers thought that dholes were responsible for the decline of various deer species, which in fact was due to overgrazing, habitat loss and poaching. Phythian Adams, a retired Indian army officer, wrote in the *Journal of the Bombay Natural History Society* in 1949, that the epithet 'a perfect swine' may with every justification be applied to the wild dog, whose nature and habits may be summed up in a single word—'bloody'. He concluded that except for his handsome appearance the wild dog does not have a single redeeming feature, and no effort, fair or foul, should be spared to destroy these pests of the jungle. As recently as 1964, E.P. Gee did speak up in favour of dholes, but in a lukewarm fashion. Dholes play a useful part in the general set up of nature, he said. They keep the deer on the move, and so favourite grazing areas do not become over-grazed and therefore impoverished. Otherwise, he commented, there is very little to be said in favour of these animals. Not surprisingly, the dhole was one of the much maligned and persecuted species in the Indian jungles and until 1975 it even carried a bounty on its head—even if a paltry one—of twenty rupees.

Many myths are woven around the dholes. These myths add up to making them seem almost human in their supposed malice and deviousness. One myth: dholes attack if people run away from them. I had an opportunity to explode this myth. One morning in Bandipur, I observed nine dholes coming out of the jungle to a forest road, and immediately I took cover behind a large tree. The dholes were fifty metres away and were trotting in my direction. To see their reaction to my running away from them, I came out and ran in full view of them, to a tree thirty metres away, which I could easily climb. The dholes, instead of chasing me, abruptly turned back with a short alarm growl, and disappeared into the bush.

Another myth is that the dhole hunts its prey in relays. According to this theory one dhole runs after the prey till it is tired and then another dhole pursues the prey and this change of hunters goes on until the prey is too exhausted to run. Thereafter, all the dholes join together and kill the prey. I never observed this to happen. Of the forty-eight chases I witnessed in Bandipur, in forty-four the dholes chased their prey for only 500 metres; only twice did the chase go beyond 500 metres. Teamwork and speed enabled them to kill their prey within short distances. It would be impossible for one dhole to pursue one particular prey for a long distance through the dense Indian jungle where there are many individuals of different prey species and different prey signs confuse the animal chasing.

I observed that dholes employ two strategies. One, which I observed while sitting up in the rosewood tree, was to flush prey to waiting dholes. The other was to go in an extended line through the forest and attack at once, alone, without flushing prey out, when suitable prey is located. It is possible to identify which strategy dholes adopt only at the beginning of the hunt, as at the end, in the melee, it would be impossible to differentiate the two strategies.

It is believed that dholes urinate on the eyes of the prey, making them blind, and then kill them. This is as improbable a technique as would be keeping butter on the head of a pond heron and catching the bird when the butter melts and blinds the bird! It is also reported that dholes urinate on leafy branches, force the prey to run into the branches, make them blind and then kill them. This again is an impossible technique for a dense jungle and I saw no evidence of this.

The reason dholes are called 'bloody' is that they kill much larger prey by biting off chunks of meat and by evisceration. Often killing occurs in daytime, witnessed by people. One March evening, atop the shooting hide when darkness was just gathering, my attention was abruptly drawn to a silent struggle between a large chital stag with a fine set of hard antlers and a group of seven dholes. Two or three dholes were biting and hanging on to the rump of the stag, thereby rendering it completely immobile, while others attacked its flanks. The stag was trying to fight off the dholes by swinging its great antlers, which never came in contact with the dholes. Through out the struggle the dholes remained silent while the deer cried out its agony three times.

Suddenly one dhole caught the snout of the stag and pulled it forward while those at the rump continued to bite and pull it backwards. Eventually the helpless stag was dragged down and the dholes started eating it even before it had died. Although predation is as much a biological process as grazing, to a layman such a sight is repugnant and bloodthirsty. However dholes are biologically predators and since they lack the killing bite of the large cats they can at best kill prey larger than themselves only by biting off chunks of meat. As blood loss and shock rapidly lower the prey's resistance, the animal thus weakened becomes easier to overcome. Close examination of numerous fresh kills clearly shows that dholes are particular about holding on to the nose of stags sporting hard antlers, obviously to prevent themselves from being stabbed by these lethal weapons. Often, in the process of biting off chunks of flesh from the rump of adult stags, dholes bite off the scrotum: this has led to the belief that dholes intentionally emasculate their prey. This too is a misapprehension. Faced with smaller prey like hare and chital fawn, dholes instantaneously kill them with one bite and a vigorous head shake.

One cloudy evening I was atop the shooting hide and heard repeated chital alarm calls and sounds of some other animals. I saw three dholes, which stood facing west, as if to intercept an animal. Soon a big chital fawn, chased by another dhole, came running in the direction of the three waiting dholes. The fawn, when it saw the dholes, veered to the right, but the dholes also swiftly moved as if to block its way. Then the fawn leaped across the dholes. When it landed six to eight metres away from the dholes, all four of them fell on it almost simultaneously. There was only a short muffled scream. Within a minute the fawn's entrails were thrown out and by this time the entire pack was on the kill.

Dholes, though they look like dogs, do not bark. The most interesting call of the dhole is a whistle. How it produces the sound is an enigma. The whistle call can be imitated by blowing into a medium-bore empty rifle cartridge and in the past hunters used to trick dholes by mimicking the call and drawing dholes closer to shoot them. Dholes separated from the rest of their pack whistle to reassemble after an unsuccessful hunt and even lone dholes whistle to discover the whereabouts of its pack members. I never observed dholes whistling to maintain the cohesiveness of their pack while the hunt was in progress. Sounds play an important role in the lives of dholes and they can be attracted, not only by imitating their whistle, but also by blowing air with a leaf between the lips thus producing a shrill note similar to the distress call of a deer fawn.

Like most other large carnivores, the dhole has an amazing ability to consume large quantities of meat. A pack of fifteen could easily eat a yearling sambar male of 90–100 kilograms, each dhole consuming about five kilograms of meat, which is a little over one fourth the body weight of the dhole. This capacity to gorge is thought to enable them to live without food for a few days: this, however, has not been verified in the field. Once I managed to collect almost all the kills made by my study pack for about fifteen days and calculated that during this period, on the average, each dhole ate 1.8 kg meat. One of the benefits of pack life, in addition to providing the capability to bring down large prey several times heavier than a single dhole, is the efficiency with which kills are eaten. Even the bones and skin of young and smaller prey are eaten. When larger kills are made, the dholes may come back even to scavenge on the dry skin. This habit of scavenging also enables dholes to appropriate kills of leopards and tigers and on many occasions leopards have actually lost their kills to dholes. Stealing of kills from other large sympatric predators can be dangerous. I have seen once a dhole pup, nearly six months old, killed and partly eaten by a leopard; the potential robber had become a prey.

One fear about the dhole is that a high density of its population can suppress tiger and leopard populations. This need not be true, as there are several behavioural and ecological parameters which help these predators to avoid conflict with one another. There is temporal and spatial variation in their use of habitat. Dholes are largely diurnal while tigers and leopards prefer to be nocturnal. The shy tiger and leopard generally avoid open habitats and dholes use them without any inhibition. Tigers generally prefer prey heavier than 100 kilograms while the leopard and dhole largely kill prey around and less than fifty kilograms. K. Ullas Karanth, the tiger specialist, has observed this kind of prey selection in Nagarahole National Park, which is adjacent to the Bandipur Tiger Reserve. In Bandipur dholes showed a preference for male sambar and male chital and my limited experience of sambar and chital kills of tigers and leopards seemed to suggest their preference for female sambar and chital. Females, which spend considerable time in cover to give birth and nurse fawns, are more prone to stalking predators like the tiger and leopard. In addition the kill data also suggest that the dhole, a coursing predator, kills mainly young or old animals while the tiger and leopard, as they hunt by stealth and surprise, can kill prey of all ages.

All dholes look alike to a casual observer. Attentive and prolonged observation, however, can help us differentiate a few individuals based on variations in their colour, and shape of the ear and tail. 'Bent Ear' was one such individual I grew to recognise. My first prolonged meeting with him was on 4 January 1977 when I went to the dhole den at around eleven in the morning. Bent Ear had already returned from the hunt and was resting in front of the den. The leaf litter was so dry I found it difficult to walk without making a noise. My approach had alerted him and pricking his left ear he looked in the direction of the sound. I crawled to the cover of a rock forty metres from the den, and, lying under a bush, I observed him.

He had an unusually thick neck and a pale white throat, chest and belly. His tail had a bend as if it had been broken. His scrotum hung loosely, showing he was aged. Throughout the three hours of observation he was suspicious of my presence but never came close to investigate. This was probably because of his dislike for the hot sun, which scorched the shadeless areas. When I left the den he was sleeping in the shade. The rustle in the bush made him raise his head lazily and open his eyes a little, but he again fell into a deep slumber to while away the hot afternoon.

Thereafter I observed him several times. He appeared to be the leader of the pack and was extremely fond of the pups.

When the pack had made a kill of a small animal the pups would run to him pestering him to regurgitate extra meat. I soon developed a strange affection for this aged hunter who flitted freely through the forest. He led a daring life. Alone and unafraid he slipped without any hesitation through the thickets which I entered with much reluctance, with bated breath and a tense body. When he suddenly disappeared in April 1978 I felt a pang of sadness which stayed with me for a long time.

During my study in Bandipur I came to understand the mechanisms of pack size regulation. During the first year of my study in the month of November, just prior to the birth of some pups, the pack of fifteen was suddenly reduced to seven or eight animals. This was unexpected. The diminished pack had three females but one gave birth to eight pups. Also, at no time were two packs seen operating in the same area, which suggests that the dholes could be territorial. I realised that mortality, and emigration of a part of the pack before the arrival of pups, breeding by one female, and the dhole's territorial nature may be the mechanisms that regulate pack and population size. In spite of these mechanisms sometimes pack sizes of twenty to twenty-five dholes are reported. Arun Venkataraman, who has done several years of research on dholes in Mudumalai Wildlife Sanctuary near Bandipur, explains that such large packs could be caused by the absence of suitable areas nearby for the emigrants to occupy.

In Bandipur the pups remained in the den until they were

seventy to eighty days old and during this time they did not visit the nearby waterholes. They possibly got enough water from mother's milk and the meat regurgitated by several of the pack members. I also observed that pups were shifted from one den to another when people disturbed the dens.

The pack cared for the pups even after they had left the den and the adults treated them with special concern and solicitude until they were four to five months old. During this period the adults would hunt either very early in the morning or late in the evening to avoid both the presence of man and the heat of the day. The pups were left in hiding during these hunts and the absence of a couple of adults in the hunting party even suggested that some adults stayed behind to guard them. Even when the pups started following the pack on hunts, one or two adults escorted young stragglers. Pups were permitted to monopolise small kills like chital fawns and when food was insufficient the adults, who had eaten earlier, regurgitated meat for them. When the pups were about seven months old, on occasion when food was insufficient, adults were reluctant to regurgitate meat. The pups, however, chased the adults and appealingly nibbled the corners of the adults' mouths until food was regurgitated.

One heavily foggy winter morning I made my way to a large tamarind tree about 500 metres south-east of Bandipur. Perched on the tree, I heard the hushed scream of a sambar fawn 150–200 metres from Bandipur village, an obvious sign of a kill. I hurried to the place, which a flock of jungle crows had already reached. Jungle crows in Bandipur tenaciously follow dholes to feed on the kill remains and were of immense help to me in locating dholes. I waited to give sufficient time to the dholes to settle on the kill as I wanted to approach them and take some photographs.

The crows were sitting on the top of a dead tree, looking down and cawing. Minutes ticked by and abruptly the dholes growled and ran in different directions. For a moment I thought that there was a fight among themselves, which had made them disperse, and as I waited for them to reassemble the crows landed on the kill site: evidence that the dholes were not at the kill. I went ahead cautiously. The crows flew up the dead tree when I approached them, and except for the splattered blood and hair and a few splinters of bone, there was no sign of a kill on the short green grass. I walked around the kill site and found on the dew covered grass, tracks of two persons who had come from and gone back to Bandipur village. Anger swelled in me when I realised that the kill probably had been stolen. The clearly visible tracks led me to a Kuruba tribal hut on the outskirts of Bandipur village. Some jungle crows were sitting on the grass rooftop of the hut and cawing, and other crows were flying around. All this clearly indicated that the kill was hidden somewhere either inside or near the hut. The Kuruba family and their neighbours, however, denied having any association with the kill.

One of the major objectives of my study was to evaluate the impact of dhole predation on chital and sambar and therefore every kill was valuable to me. I realised I had to report the stolen kill to the forest department to put an end to this illegal activity. I went to the office of the Range Forest Officer in Bandipur village and lodged a complaint. The Range Forest Officer was aware of the problem of local people stealing kills. I was able to convince him that such stealing, if unabated, could seriously affect my study and also the delicate prey-predator balance that exists in Bandipur Tiger Reserve. Determined to put an end to this disturbance, he accompanied me with two guards to the hut of the tribal. An intensive search brought out a thirty kilogram sambar fawn wrapped in sacks hidden in one corner of the hut. I removed the jaw of the fawn for ageing it by studying tooth emption, and pieces of lung and liver for an investigation of parasitism. We left the carcass at the kill site in the fervent hope that the dholes would come back to feed on it.

Since time immemorial, in every association with man, the dhole has been the loser. Jungle tribes all over the range of dholes have been following dholes and appropriating their kills down the years. Given this parasitic association tribes such as Gonds in Madhya Pradesh never harm dholes directly. Another way in which dholes are harmed by people is by den-digging and killing pups. This happens most in areas where dholes prey on livestock. In such areas carcasses of livestock killed by dholes are also poisoned. For example, Lieutenant Colonel R.W. Burton in an article written in 1941 in the *Journal of the Bombay Natural History Society*, recommends the use of Strychnine bihydrochloride for poisoning dholes.

Burton thought that as the stock of deer in all parts of the country was rapidly lessening, it should be the policy of the Imperial Forest Department to offer sufficient government rewards to encourage the continual destruction of wild dogs in all Reserve forests. This was practised throughout India but only certain agencies kept a record of how many dholes were killed.

For twenty-one years, from 1912, the average yearly destruction of dholes in the area controlled by the Nilgiri Game Association in South India numbered thirty-eight and the reward offered for each dhole killed was Rs 20: which was a covetable amount in those days. This promotion of killing was continued by the Association and between 1939 and 1964, 309 dholes were slayed.

Fortunately for the dholes, the tide has turned. The last dhole was shot in Bandipur in 1975 and being in Schedule II of the Indian Wildlife Act 1972, the dhole is now totally protected from hunting. Unless there is permission from the Chief Wildlife Warden of the state, the dhole cannot be legally shot. Neither wildlife managers nor conservationists believe any longer in the accusation that dhole can suppress tiger populations. Since the inception of Project Tiger, many tiger habitats such as Kanha, Melghat, Simlipal, Bandipur and Periyar, which also harbour dholes, have shown a significant increase in tiger numbers—which would not have happened had the dholes been containing tiger numbers.

My study on dholes in Bandipur Tiger Reserve from 1976 to 1978 was fraught with discomfort and dangers. One major problem was my allergy to ticks, which were abundant in the jungle. Initially the tick bites led to fever and itching, and, though eventually the fever stopped, the itching continued and I never developed immunity to the bites. Some of the bites itched for months. The healed bites, which were all over my body, were black. Soon I looked as if I had had a serious attack of small-pox. Dangers from elephants were many. Once, while looking for kills, I walked into a sleeping cow elephant in a dense scrub and mistook it for dead! I foolishly made horrendous sounds by beating two sticks of dead and dry bamboo to verify whether the elephant was dead; the cow came out charging with her tiny calf on her heels. I was in my early thirties then and had the confidence that I could run and escape elephants. This confidence, which enabled me to escape from two very bad chases by elephants, was shattered when a Conservator of Forests, who was accompanying me, was tragically killed by a young tusker. Thereafter for several weeks I walked with great fear in my heart. Any rustle caused by a heavy-bodied animal in the bush sent a chill up my spine.

I spent over five thousand enjoyable hours in the jungle

and observed dholes for a little over a hundred hours. My project was the first Ph.D study by an Indian biologist on a free ranging large mammal. Nearly twenty-five years have passed since my field study and there are many questions that need to be answered to fully understand dhole biology and ecology. Some of them are: What prevents *Cuon alpinus primaevus* from returning to prey-rich areas like Corbett Tiger Reserve? What diseases periodically wipe out dholes in Reserves like Kanha and how are these diseases transmitted? What happens to the migrants and what is their social status? What is the genetic status of the different dhole populations? Several short term studies focusing on different populations of dholes and a long term study of three or four neighbouring packs in an expansive dhole habitat, with several dholes individually marked and some radio-collared, are urgently required to unravel many of the existing mysteries about the dhole.

4 🌿 The Tahr Hills

We had walked a whole summer day in May, from Thirukkurangudi village to Thulukkamparai River, at the base of the 'tahr hills'. A large flat rock on the bank of the river was our halting place for the night. In the evening, while the others were busy bringing wood for the fire and cooking food, I scanned the surrounding slopes with binoculars. Towards sunset, I was rewarded with the sighting of a large brown male tahr on a precipitous slope. It watched us as we prepared for the night.

The Thiruvannamalai hills, with its two peaks, the southern and the northern, ranging in altitude from 1500 to 1750 metres, are at the southern end of the Western Ghats. They harbour the southernmost population of the Nilgiri Tahr—the endangered wild goat. The area is now within the Kalakad Mundanthurai Tiger Reserve but in 1976, when I surveyed the tahr population there, it wasn't. I had gone with my younger

brother Sekar and three local assistants when E.R.C. Davidar, a renowned Indian naturalist who had been compiling information on Nilgiri tahr distribution, called for help.

Early the next morning, while the grey junglefowl were still crowing from their roosts, we climbed further up. The hidden boulders among the tall grass (*Themeda cymbaria* and *Cymbopogon flexuosus*) and *Phoenix humilis* bushes made the route treacherous. Around seven in the morning, while negotiating a steep ridge on the northern peak, we saw a female tahr with a young kid. The climb then took us through a patch of evergreen forest for about forty-five minutes, before we reached the southern peak where the new grass was short and green, and tahr pellets abundant. As we went around looking for tahr and other wildlife, at around eight, at a short distance, we saw a group of nine men on a meadow near a spring. Smoke rose from a wood fire.

Seeing us, the men panicked. We were unexpected visitors. One man ran with two guns to hide them behind a large rock. We ambled up looking as casual as possible and began a conversation, trying to put them at ease. We had to know what was going on. Eventually, we confirmed that they had come to poach tahr. That morning, they had shot three of a thirty-strong herd, but had been able to collect only two. The third dead tahr had fallen into a deep gorge. Now quite relaxed, they became hospitable: they offered us the liver of the animal they had killed, which was bubbling on the fire. We took a few photographs of them with the dead tahr, but refusing the offer of a liver lunch, we traced our way back.

Returning quickly to the plains, I rushed to lodge a complaint with the Tamil Nadu Forest Department. A truckload of foresters was sent in straightaway. The poachers were caught, and fined Rs 1500. For once, I felt, I had been in the right place at the right time.

The ancestor of the Nilgiri tahr evolved in the Palaearctic zone, north of the Himalaya. Eventually, a population of primitive tahr reached the Himalaya and there, one line evolved as the Himalayan tahr; another went west and evolved as the Arabian tahr; and a third found its way to the temperate climate of the high mountains of the Western Ghats. The cooler climate in the past enabled them to cross the now arid and hot Rajasthan and Madhya Pradesh.

The tahr possibly populated all the habitable peaks in the Western Ghats in the early days, but in time, it got exterminated in the mountains north of the Nilgiris. Even in the Kalakad Mundanthurai Tiger Reserve, there were many more tahr in the 1940s. Constant poaching and competition with cattle, which were earlier penned in the mountain pastures during the summer, led to their gradual decline, and tahr disappeared from peak after peak. Now, within the Reserve, the tahr occurs only in the northern end (Kadayam hills) and in the southern hills.

Many years passed after my first visit to the tahr hills, and

I often wondered whether the wild goat of Thiruvannamalai was now being hunted by anyone other than the leopards. Did the poachers still prowl around with their guns and cooking pots? Six years later, in December 1983, I thought I would find out.

This time, on my trip to the tahr hills, I was accompanied by Pramod Kant, the Warden of Kalakad Wildlife Sanctuary, Dr Clifford Rice, an American wildlife biologist who had just completed his study of tahr in Eravikulam National Park, and Ajay Desai and N. Sivaganesan, researchers from the Bombay Natural History Society. Jothi, our tracker, suggested that we should walk towards a cave, which would be shelter for the night, and we could look for tahr the next day. As we climbed the hills, the sky was overcast and the drizzle incessant.

Jothi's 'cave', just a slanting rock at 900 metres, was at the base of the northern peak. The cave faced east, and would have been suitable for camping during the south-west monsoon, but during the north-east monsoon, which was the cause of the current drizzle, it was open to the wind and water. Before sunset, unmindful of the rain, we wandered around and saw many fresh tahr pellets. Then we settled in for the night, wet to the bone. The wind and drizzle continued. Cold and miserable, we waited for the sun, but the next day it went on raining. We had to admit defeat and descended to the plains. On the way, however, we were pleased to see the fresh pugmarks of a tigress in the shelter of another 'cave' 300 metres below.

Years passed, and the memory of the silent, watchful tahr remained. The urge to go and see it again grew in me. Finally, in June 1990, I found my way to the tahr area yet again. Pramod Kant had come back as Field Director of the newly-established Tiger Reserve, and had made all the arrangements for my visit. Jothi was now seventy-four but was back as a part of our four-man team.

A jeep took us as far as it could go, and then we climbed for five hours to reach the cave. Along the way, an occasional drizzle came down like a threat. I wandered around that evening, scouring the place for tahr where I had seen the female with her kid in 1976 and found tahr pellets in 1983. I saw pig diggings, sambar pellets and numerous sloth bear scats with the seeds of *Phoenix humilis*. But there was no sign of tahr. Against the heavy wind, I found it difficult even to hold and focus the binoculars. My eyes, windswept, watered.

The next morning, with Jothi and a forest guard, I left for the southern peak. Reaching the shoulder of the northern peak, we sat on a vantage point and scanned the southern peak with binoculars. I sighted ten tahr, and began making my way to the southern peak. Walking through an evergreen patch, I noticed two or three day old signs of someone having cut branches in the forest. Someone had obviously been there a few days earlier. The southern peak was burnt in several places; the burn marks too were recent. I saw many signs of tahr and began longing for a good photograph.

Instructing Jothi and the guard to trail behind, I crept ahead. I approached a tahr herd till I was just a hundred metres away. An abrupt change in the wind direction revealed me to the tahr, however, which scurried up a steep ridge. My photo-op had escaped.

We began walking back to the cave, Jothi companionably chatting along. He had come to the mountains without telling his wife, he said, afraid she would prevent him from going to the tahr hills at his age. He wondered if this might be his last trip with me, and tears filled his eyes. He feared that the tahr would not survive long in their battle with the poachers. I remembered someone informing me two days earlier that a tahr had been found shot dead a month before.

We reached our cave at five in the evening. I fell asleep and woke up after two hours. Thereafter my sleep was not deep. At about eleven, the moon rose over the mountains. The wet areas of the northern peak shone in the moonlight, and the patch of evergreen forest in front of the cave looked darker. The mountains looked indestructible, and even the evergreen forest in that inaccessible area appeared safe from vandalism. I wondered how long the remaining tahr would hold out against the ravages of poachers.

My most recent visit to the Thiruvannamalai hills was in early 1995. Pramod Kant was still Field Director, and we decided to trek to the tahr area. Meanwhile, there were rumours that the tahr had been heavily poached by illegal *ganja*

(*Cannabis sativa*) cultivators, who had a camp in the evergreen forest. Walking the whole day, we reached a vantage point on the northern ridge, from where I could see the northern aspect of the southern ridge. The grass there had been burnt a few weeks earlier, and there was already a new flush of green. The forest staff that had gone a few weeks earlier to destroy the *ganja* cultivation had seen seven tahr. We saw a large group of bonnet macaque that was feeding and playing. But there was no tahr. We spent the night on the northern ridge, watching a full moon rise, traverse across a cloudless sky crowded with stars, and eventually set.

There is still hope for the long-term conservation of tahr in the Kalakad Mundanthurai Tiger Reserve. My recent surveys show that there is a population of about fifty tahr near Upper Kothayar, which is about ten kilometres north-west of the Thiruvannamalai hills, as the crow flies. The tahr habitat in the southern Western Ghats is still continuous, and extends from the Thiruvannamalai hills to the southern slopes of the Agastyarmalai in the west, and to the Kannunni-Kottangathatti peaks in the north. Agastyarmalai is the tallest mountain (1866 metres) in this area. If the Thiruvannamalai and Upper Kothayar populations of tahr are closely protected against poachers and cattle, and the grasslands are managed by controlled burning, the tahr population could increase in number, and five hundred to a thousand tahr could easily thrive in this expansive habitat.

5   The Leap of the Goat Antelope

An episode that I particularly liked in Jim Corbett's *The Maneaters of Kumaon* describes the hunting of goral. Corbett was on the trail of the Champawat maneater. Camping in Pati village (Corbett calls it Pali), he asked the villagers whether he could be led to goral, promising to take one for his camp and two for the village. Three men from the village readily agreed and took the hunter to a ridge where goral was said to be plentiful. The four of them sat under a tree at the base of the ridge, watching the slope. Soon, a movement nearly 200 metres up the ridge attracted Corbett's attention.

It turned out to be a goral watching them. Corbett lay down, held his rifle against the root of an oak tree, took aim at the white throat of the goral, and fired from an uncomfortable angle. The villagers saw no movement on the slope and concluded that Corbett had mistakenly shot at a dry bush. Moments later,

a goral materialised from out of cover and began sliding and rolling downward. This disturbed two more goral, which jumped over the bushes, stood still for a few seconds sounding their characteristic wheezing alarm, and then ran along the slope. Corbett swiftly shot them down one after the other. All three goral rolled down and reached the tree where the party was sitting.

The villagers were so impressed by this performance that they later spread the story that Corbett's magic bullet not only killed the hidden goral but also brought them down to the place where he was waiting. Corbett became an instant hero, winning the confidence of the villagers who thereafter willingly followed him into maneater terrain.

Interesting, if meagre, information on the goral emerges from this episode. They live in small groups, rest under cover in the heat of the noon, and when alarmed, run for a short distance before standing still to sound the alarm. This little knowledge stoked my curiosity. I wanted to see much more of the goral for myself, and know more about it.

When I joined the Wildlife Institute of India in March 1985, what I wanted to do right away was to see the goral in its natural habitat. In December 1986, I was camping in Dholkhand in the Rajaji National Park, almost adjacent to the Institute. One morning, I suggested to my colleague G.S. Rawat, a man with immense experience in the Himalaya, that we explore the high ridge in front of the Dholkhand forest bungalow, which looked to me like perfect goral habitat. We clambered up the slope, and within two hours saw five goral.

There was no time for the goral during our work hours. We decided we'd do a private study of it in the Park on weekends and on other holidays. When we explained our plans to S.P. Goyal, another colleague, who before joining the Institute had climbed only as high as the sand dunes of the Thar desert, he decided to join us, and we began working as a team. We named the area Goral Ridge.

The goral is a stocky goat-like animal 65 to 70 centimetres at the shoulder and 20 to 25 kilograms in weight. Both sexes have horns and a conspicuous white throat patch. It is difficult to distinguish between the sexes from a distance. There are, however, some differences in their horns. The male's horns are thicker at the base, and when viewed from the front, more divergent than those of females. Taxonomists have placed the goral in a group popularly known as 'goat-antelopes' (Tribe *Rupicaprini*), said to be the common ancestor of both goats and sheep. The tribe seems to have an Asian origin. The roughly ten million-year-old *Pachygazella grangeri* of the Pliocene, which is found in fossil deposits in China, was the probable ancestor of the rupicaprines. The *Rupicaprini* once had an extensive distribution in Eurasia and possibly in Africa. For example, in the past, a large goral, *Gallogoral meneghinii*, lived in the areas around present day Italy. Living relatives of the goral are the serow, *Nemorhaedus sumatraensis*, of south-east Asia, Taiwan and Japan; the Rocky Mountain goat, *Oreamnos americanus*, of North America; and the chamois, *Rupicapra rupicapra*, of Europe.

The goral has a wide distribution, from the Indus Kohistan region in the western Himalaya in Pakistan, across the eastern Himalaya, Myanmar, Thailand, China and in a few scattered areas in South Korea, North Korea, eastern Russia and the adjoining regions of China. Along this arc, which is discontinuous now, there are several species and subspecies. Within the Himalayan region of the Indian subcontinent, there are three species: the Himalayan goral (*Nemorhaedus goral,* with two subspecies: grey goral *N.g. bedfordi* in the western Himalaya, and ·brown goral *N.g.goral* in the eastern Himalaya), Evan's long-tailed goral (*N. caudatus evansi* in Nagaland and possibly in Assam) and Burmese red goral (*N. baileyi cranbrooki* in northeast Arunachal Pradesh). Both Evan's long-tailed goral and Burmese red goral are found in Myanmar. Thailand has one species (Evan's long-tailed goral). China has four subspecies: Chinese long-tailed goral (*N.c.caudatus)* Tibetan red goral *N. baileyi baileyi*, Grey long-tailed goral *(N.c.griseus)* and Korean or Amur long-tailed goral (*N. c. raddeanus*). Amur goral occurs in North Korea, South Korea and the Russian montane forests along the border with China and the coastal cliffs overlooking the sea of Japan.

In India, the goral is found in the Himalaya and Shivaliks of Kashmir, Himachal Pradesh, Uttaranchal, Sikkim, West

Bengal and Arunachal Pradesh. It is also reported to occur in the state of Nagaland and Assam. Gorals inhabit altitudes varying from 200 metres in the Uttaranchal Shivaliks, to 4000 metres in the Garhwal Himalaya. There could be 100,000 gorals in the Indian Himalaya. The action plan for Caprinae, compiled by the World Conservation Union (IUCN), reports that poaching is the single major problem threatening the goral throughout its range.

Similar to the goral is the Japanese serow, and it is worth studying how the Japanese have dealt with problems like poaching in relation to the serow. In India the serow occurs in the northeast, central and western Himalaya, ranging in altitude from 1000 metres in the states of Manipur and Meghalaya, to 4000 metres in Himachal Pradesh and Uttaranchal. There are over fifty protected areas in the serow's range, varying from 4 km² to 1800 km². Of the roughly 19,000 kms² of serow habitat (sub-alpine zone) in India, 6000–8000 kms² are in protected areas.

Not bad at first glance. But several problems remain, and even continue to grow—habitat fragmentation, habitat disturbance by mushroom and medicinal plant collectors, and poaching. Serow habitat lies in inaccessible areas where protection is hard to enforce; most of the locals relish serow meat and have been hunting serow for ages. Therefore we have a situation in India which is somewhat similar to the one in Japan at the beginning of this century.

One difference, which could be critical, is predation. In Japan, the black bear is the only natural predator of serow. But most serow areas in India have leopards, and some at higher altitudes even have snow leopards. A few areas have tigers and clouded leopards. Areas like Namdapha in Arunachal Pradesh may have all four cats. All these areas may also have black bear. The consequences of a combination of poaching and predation could be disastrous for the territorial serow, which occurs at low densities.

The Japanese serow was hunted traditionally for its meat and pelt. As a result of long-term unrestricted hunting, its population declined. Coupled with this was loss of habitat. By the early 1900s, serows were found only in high altitude zones. In order to arrest this worrying trend, the conservation-minded Japanese government, even as early as 1934, designated the serow a 'natural monument', and in 1955 it became a 'special natural monument'.

A large-scale afforestation scheme was in progress when the serow was designated as a special natural monument. From 1955 to 1973, 3000 kms^2 of natural forest was cut down every year and converted to coniferous forest. Early in the 1970s, the area of this artificial forest exceeded 90,000 kms^2, 35 per cent of Japan's total forest area. Plantations in the early and pre-thicket stages, which last till the trees are seven to ten years old, are habitat preferred by the serow, for the abundant cover and high quality food.

In the absence of poaching, the serow immediately responded to this habitat improvement. Its range expanded considerably and populations shot up—from 75,000 in 1980 to 100,000 in 1985. The expansion of the range and population, however, had a disastrous effect on the plantations, especially those of the *Hinoki cypress*, which is the mainstay of the Japanese timber industry. As a result, a new conservation strategy was formulated to manage serow. Thirteen serow protection areas, ranging in size from 1400 kms^2 to 2150 kms^2 were designated as natural monuments. Outside these areas, serow control through hunting was permitted. In two districts where damage to plantations was serious, 4000 serow were shot.

But it was not a mindless massacre. The carcasses were examined to collect information on food habits (by analysing the stomach contents), nutritional condition, age structure and fecundity of the population. The culling programme was coupled with extensive research on both captive and wild animals, using radio telemetry. As a result, the Japanese serow is today one of the most extensively studied species in Asia. This research has obviously benefited conservation programmes for the Japanese serow, but the knowledge can be applied to other serow species and the goral too.

Our own research resulted in the collection of much new data on the goral, hitherto a little known species. Goral are primarily grazers, although they feed upon tender shoots of certain shrubs and herbs when available. On Goral Ridge, we observed that when langurs (*Semnopithecus entellus*) were feeding up in the trees, the goral tended to gather below, feeding on fallen leaves, flowers and fruits. We have also seen sambar (*Cervus unicolor*), chital (*Axis axis*) and barking deer (*Muntiacus muntjak*) join goral in such situations. On rainy days, goral can be seen throughout the day. In winter, however, there appears to be a morning and evening peak in feeding. The animals tend to rest for the remaining part of the day, and if the weather is cool, they can be seen basking. In summer, goral retreat into cover as early as 7.30 in the morning, emerging only late in the evening when the heat has died down. When thirsty, however, they visit waterholes even in the heat of the noonday sun, usually choosing a water source close to steep ridges.

Approximately 60 per cent of our goral sightings were of solitary animals, or of females accompanied by a yearling and/ or a kid. The largest group comprised seven animals, which rested on a gentle slope after feeding on the lush monsoon grass. We frequently came across pugmarks of leopards and tigers on Goral Ridge. Our analysis of tiger scats (droppings) indicated that the large but agile tiger does occasionally prey on the nimble-footed goral.

Walking transects, and wandering over the hilly tract of Rajaji National Park, which is around 300 kms², we estimated that there were about a thousand goral in the Park. The Ganga, however, divides the population. West of the Ganga the best concentrations appeared to be in two areas, the Dholkhand and the Bom Dhera ridges. Both areas are free from cattle grazing and lopping, a scourge all through the Park. Both locations also have water in the valley, even in summer, but they suffer the problem of *bhabar* grass (*Euliopsis binata*) cutting by villagers in winter. Fortunately, poaching is not a major problem here, a fact that is reflected in the high density of sambar and barking deer.

One benefit of cutting the grass in winter is the increased availability of protein-rich tender grasses in summer, a boon to ungulates. The Shivalik habitat could probably do with some form of resource manipulation, like the controlled burning of grasses, in order to provide more nutritious food for wild ungulates in summer. But grass cutting by villagers, which seems impossible to control, has two conservation problems. First, the grass-cutters steal predator kills all through the winter, and second, rolling grass bundles from hilltops causes a lot of erosion in the fragile Shivaliks. Grass cutting, along with other disturbances such as cattle grazing and poaching, can gradually lead to the decline of prey and predators.

Our studies in Rajaji inspired two of our students, Charudutt Mishra and Anand Pendharkar, both nimble-footed like goral, to research this mountain goat for their M.Sc. dissertations. Charu carried out his study in the Majathal Wildlife Sanctuary, and Anand in the Simbalbara Wildlife Sanctuary (both in Himachal Pradesh) and the adjacent Darpur

Reserved forest in Haryana. Charu found that goral fed almost entirely on grass. In his study area, goral preferred open areas with good grass cover, and avoided shrub-rich patches, particularly those where the height of the shrubs exceeded the shoulder height of the goral. The goral was partial to steep slopes at angles of roughly thirty degrees. Anand observed that the animal was not particularly social. Females were comparatively more social, and males associated with female groups only during the breeding period in November.

Over my long years of field research, I have discovered that animals seldom see people if they remain hidden in trees, and to me, waiting in the trees to sight goral and take a picture of this little-photographed goat, was much more exciting than crouching in a ground hide. I made myself a simple hide up in a *Mallotus philippinensis* tree in the valley, hardly fifteen metres from a slushy area near a natural salt lick, which was frequented by goral during the hot hours in summer. I have taken some good pictures sitting in this tree hide, and recorded some interesting observations on the behaviour of goral.

However, I got more pleasure from waiting and photographing goral from two small trees at the top of Goral Ridge. In course of time, I realised that photography was possible only in summer, late in the evening, when the goral left the cool cover of the valley and came to the top of the ridge to feed. This, however, necessitated a steep climb for me at around two in the afternoon, when it was exceedingly hot. An *Ougeinia oojeinensis* tree at the edge of the ridge-top, and a *Grewia elastica* tree about ten metres away, near a trail frequently used by goral, gave me the necessary hideouts on the ridge-top.

Once I plucked and threw down some leaves of the *O. oojeinensis* tree for a better view. The leaf of *O. oojeinensis*, a leguminous species, is reported to be highly nutritious, and when I was waiting on this tree, a female goral appeared and began feeding on the leaves I had dropped. She was so close I could have jumped on to her back! In spite of these close encounters, I eventually gave up sitting on this tree for it swayed unnervingly even in a light wind. I was afraid that a heavy wind might uproot the tree altogether, and a straight fall of fifty metres or so would turn my adventure into a fatal accident.

Watching goral in the afternoon was an exquisite mingling of pain and pleasure. The temperature soared over 40°C one day as I made my way up the ridge. I had to keep stopping to rest and found the animal world doing the same: passing a dense patch of *Bauhinia vahlii* along the ridge, I flushed two gorals resting in the shade; a short while later, a sambar doe with a yearling hind and a fawn, resting in the scanty shade of trees, ran out of the cover and went up the hill. By the time I settled down in my hide amidst the foliage, it was around three in the afternoon. Afternoons can be eerily silent. I could almost hear myself breathe.

When the sun began to set, I noticed a palpable change in the mood of the jungle. A steady cool breeze made the branches sway. Several animals seemed to wake from their slumber. A group of sambar and even an elephant bull appeared out of nowhere, and began to feed on the valley vegetation. The alarm calls of chital, sambar and barking deer all around the ridge indicated that the predators had shaken themselves awake too.

I heard the distinct footsteps of a goral on the dry leaf litter as it slowly made its way up from its resting site through the forest, towards the grass-covered slope, which I faced. It was a male, and he fed peacefully on the tender shoots of the understorey vegetation. When he reached the grassy strip, he began to gorge on the green leaves of a bamboo-like grass, *Neyraudia arundinacea*, and the sprouting shoots of *bhabar* grass. I sat without any movement amidst the foliage and allowed him to approach within five metres of me, and surprised him by taking a photograph. The sound of the camera startled him, and he ran away from me, leaping effortlessly twenty metres down the steep slope. He then stood looking in my direction, stamping his forefoot and whistling his alarm to the jungle at large. I froze till he nervously resumed feeding.

When the sun touched the horizon, I decided to leave. If there were no elephants on the way, it would take me around forty minutes to reach the Dholkhand forest bungalow. I did not worry too much about elephants: by now I knew how to avoid them if they crossed my path. But terrorists from Punjab were supposed to have taken shelter in the Rajaji National

Park then. While I could dodge elephants, I had no idea how to avoid armed and desperate men. I found it ironical that of all the imagined dangers of the wilds, the ones I feared most were from my own species.

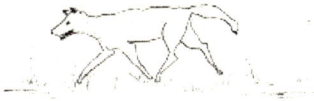

6   The Vanishing Tiger

I was perched upon a tamarind tree close to Sulli *katte*, a pond in Bandipur Wildlife Sanctuary. The branch I was sitting on moved with the wind, bringing about a benign sense of pastoral calm within me. But a jungle is an unpredictable place. The thundery air was suddenly shot through with excited alarm calls of langur, chital and sambar. They were coming from the lantana patch between the roads to Chamanahalla and Ministerguthi. Having started my field study on dholes only two months before, I thought the alarm calls indicated the presence of dholes. I hurried down the tree and ran towards the Chamanahalla road, half an eye and ear out for elephants. The alarm calls persisted and the location of the predator was indicated by an excited group of langur up in a grove of tall trees amidst the lantana, hardly sixty metres from the road. I walked from the road to the edge of the lantana, stood behind a large tree and waited. The alarm calls persisted. I took out a medium-bore empty rifle cartridge, which I always carried with me when I did my field study on dholes, and blew into it to mimic the whistling call of the dhole. I expected some response from the dholes. Instead, there was a terrifying roar and the sound of a heavy animal running through the dense bushes some thirty metres to my left. Hidden behind the tree, I peeped out to see what it was. Before me was my first wild tiger, ears laid flat, snarling and growling fiercely. It stood for a few seconds, looking around trying to locate the 'dhole' that had whistled. I froze behind the tree, and the tiger retreated into the dense growth, not seeing me. I walked back to Bandipur in the gathering darkness. It was 6 September 1976 and the sight would be engraved on my mind forever.

E.P. Gee, an English tea planter who lived in Assam, devoted his money, time and energy to the study and conservation of Indian wildlife. He made the first 'guesstimate' of the tiger population in India: around 1900, according to Gee, there were about 40,000 tigers in India. In 1947, Jim Corbett wrote in *Maneaters of Kumaon* that the Himalayan foothills had had ten times more tigers than that, ie about 400,000, when he learnt to hunt there as a boy in the late nineteenth century. Earlier hunting records vouch for this. Maharaja Kumar of Udaipur shot at least a thousand tigers in his lifetime, and the Maharaja of Surguja's score topped Udaipur's by a hundred and fifty.

In the USA, Canada, Zimbabwe and South Africa, hunting

has been used to help conservation. India, however, has neglected this aspect of wildlife management. Wealthy hunters from India and abroad hunted animals for sport but did little in return to keep alive populations of the animals they hunted. Meanwhile, improved health care enabled the human population to increase rapidly, resulting in the loss of more and more tiger habitat to agriculture and developmental projects. Crop protection guns were easily available, and poaching became uncontrollable. Villagers began to poison the carcasses of cattle killed by tiger. This was by far the greatest danger to tiger populations; while legal hunting was selective, and poachers usually shoot a single animal, poisoning can eradicate entire families of tigers that feed on the poisoned carcasses. Such surreptitious poisoning also depleted numerous other carnivores like hyenas and jackals, which often scavenge on tiger kills.

Tiger hunting was banned in India in 1969. By 1972, India's tiger population had dwindled to 1,827. In 1973, Project Tiger, a national campaign with international tentacles, was launched to save the tiger. Initially, nine reserves were selected, covering an area of 16,314 km^2, and representing diverse biogeographic zones. The objective was to protect and manage ecosystems in which the tiger lives, with the ultimate objective of allowing an increase in the population of the tiger and other associated species.

The initial years of Project Tiger were full of optimism,

enthusiasm and action. Villages in crucial tiger habitat were resettled outside. Protection to the habitat and all forms of wildlife became more vigorous. Kanha and Bandipur Tiger Reserves, for example, secured nearly 800 km² each, exclusively for the tiger and its co-species. Livestock in the villages inside and on the periphery of the Reserve was systematically vaccinated against communicable diseases, such as foot-and-mouth and rinderpest, that often take a heavy toll of wild ungulates when they come in contact with infected livestock. Slowly, more and more tiger reserves were added to the list, and today there are 27 tiger reserves with a total area of about 37,761 km², supporting some 1615 tigers, according to Forest Department records. In 1972, the nine tiger reserves had only 268 tigers. In 1989, tiger numbers in the country stood at 4334, and the world conservation community acclaimed Project Tiger as a conservation success story. Of the eight subspecies of the tiger, the Caspian, Javan and the Balinese are now extinct, and the south China tiger is close to extinction. Only the Indian race had managed to revive its population.

One section of the conservation community, however, doubted this success story. In their view, the 'increase' was not so much due to Project Tiger as to unscientific methods of counting. A tiger census is usually carried out by identifying individual tigers on the basis of their pug marks. There are three major problems in the use of this method. Firstly, the pug marks of the same tiger could vary significantly from substratum to substratum, and therefore tracings of the same individual on sand and mud, for example, will be different. Secondly, if three or four persons trace the same pug mark each produces a different tracing. Third, on the day of the census, a large number of untrained and unmotivated people are employed to do this exercise, leading to the collection of unreliable data. Recently, Dr K. Ullas Karanth, a leading tiger biologist, demonstrated that in high-density areas, the population could be reliably estimated using camera traps. In the Rajaji-Corbett Tiger Conservation Unit, Dr S.P. Goyal and I have demonstrated that it is possible to get reliable information on the abundance of tigers in different parts of this unit simply by counting the different pug marks along the river beds or *raus*. Such reliable methods, rather than counting each and every tiger, are needed to assess and monitor tiger numbers in different parts of the tiger's range.

While India was well aware of the trade in tiger skins, it was almost oblivious of the magnitude of the trade in tiger bone and other body parts for oriental medicine till the late 1980s. Countries like China and Taiwan use every part of the tiger in their traditional medicines. It is also reported that the Chinese use the bones for brewing liquor. In the past, the Chinese were probably able to get their supply from China itself, as the estimated south China tiger population in 1950 was around 4000. Around this period, China also had a considerable number of the 'Northeast China' tiger, better known as the Siberian or Amur tiger, and may be 2000 or so Indo-Chinese and Indian tigers. When the Chinese population came close to extinction the Chinese started to look for their supply from neighbouring Myanmar, Thailand, Laos, Cambodia and Vietnam. Once tiger numbers in these countries declined, the Chinese began looking further afield for their supply: Nepal, Bhutan and India came into the danger zone.

In the late 1980s, there were occasions when Indian forest officials unearthed tiger poaching incidents, and were surprised to find that intact skins were either abandoned or buried nearby but complete skeletons were missing. Soon it dawned upon them that there is a trade in tiger bones, which in fact fetches more money than the trade in the skin. Tiger skin in India can fetch up to Rs.10,000 each but the bones of an adult tiger, which weighs between 15 and 20 kilograms, can fetch ten times this amount (Peter Mathiessen in his *Tigers in the Snow* [2000] reports that 15 kilograms of powdered tiger bones can fetch a street price of US$ 750,000). It is also easier to travel with the bones, which are difficult to identify, than with the skin.

In the first half of 1993, investigations by TRAFFIC India— the wildlife trade monitoring arm of the World Wide Fund for Nature (WWF)—forest officials and the police, led to the seizure of 475 kilograms of tiger bones and 13 tiger skins. It was estimated that at least 30 tigers were killed for that material. In 1999, according to the Wildlife Protection Society of India, 280 kilograms of tiger bones got smuggled out of India.

Conservationists fear this is the tip of the iceberg, and at this rate of decimation, the tiger will become extinct in India within a few decades.

The enormous amounts of money involved in this racket make kingpins out of poachers, who are willing to risk a great deal to lay their hands on tiger parts. The inadequately paid, under-equipped and poorly motivated staff of the wildlife protection force are insufficient and unprepared to fight the nexus of poachers, who often kill tigers silently using poison, snares and leg-hold jaw traps. The efficiency and morale of the protection force is further weakened when they identify poachers and seek them out only to find the state unwilling to administer justice.

Better protection will come about when the lower staff in the protection force are motivated and facilitated with proper equipment for patrolling, given extra allowances and awards for exemplary service, and led by officers who set an example by their devotion to their duty. Volunteers from NGOs and forest villages could strengthen the protection force. Mobilising an effective force would be expensive: tourism resorts that prosper outside protected areas could share these costs. The law should ensure that at least one third of the revenue generated by these resorts go to the Reserve for the benefit of local people, habitat management, staff welfare and improving protection.

Ideally every Reserve should have a foundation represented by the Forest Department, representatives of local people, conservationists and resort managers, and all should work together with the single objective of improving the conservation prospects of the tiger and its habitat. Wherever tiger and elephant occur together, conservation efforts should be two-fold, and every rupee available for conservation should be usefully spent on the management of habitat. Existing wildlife corridors should be strengthened, and wherever possible, new corridors should be created. The conservation community should consistently pressurise government to pin down those behind tiger and elephant poaching. This country should demonstrate to the world that it has the capability to save the tiger and the elephant along with their enchanting jungle homes.

7   Mammoths at Love and War

The elephant bull towered by almost two feet over the tallest female in the group which grazed on the edge of the Ramganga reservoir. He hovered around courting a young adult female. His musth flow was coming to an end, as indicated by the two small wet patches and traces of dried flow down the sides of his massive head. His interest in the young adult female was conspicuous. He always kept to her side and when she waded into the reservoir he plunged in after her. A smaller and younger bull that was already in the water hastily moved away when it became apparent to him that he was between the female and the mammoth. The young bull moved around the pair in a wide circle, and eventually, discretion proving the better part of valour, he retreated from the water. In his situation we would have exerted ourselves similarly to avoid attention from the great bull. The sun had just set behind a chain of hills on the far side of the Ramganga

Big Boss, the bull elephant at Rajaji National Park.

reservoir, leaving the sky reddish gold. The glow of the fading light made the behemoth look more magnificent still. His grace, size and power mesmerised us. He was one of the members of a group of elephants we were watching on Dhikala chaur (grassland) in Corbett Tiger Reserve one evening in early May 1995.

The mammoth was fully aware of the presence of the young bull and the other members of the group, but was unconcerned about them. He submerged himself in the water alongside the female and gently nudged her. After a few minutes he waded towards the shore churning and splashing the water all along, and then heaved himself out onto dry land. The young bull, although at a distance of at least 30 metres, hurriedly moved away when the mammoth turned in his direction. The twilight was soft but bright enough for us to clearly see his long, massive tusks. The wear on the right tusk indicated that he had used it much more than the left one. As night fell, the mammoth strolled away from the group towards the forest. He walked with great dignity and poise. The extensive poaching of tuskers has made such magnificent bulls a rarity in many of the elephant ranges in India. We felt a pang when we saw him leave, wondering if we were to see him again.

Although many articles and books, both popular and scientific, have been written on Asian elephants, the life of bulls in their natural environment has not been documented for many elephant ranges. This is largely because of the paucity of research on bulls, and, to some extent, the scarcity of adult bulls in most ranges because of poaching. We studied the elephant bulls at Dhikala and gathered some fascinating information on the elephant bulls of Corbett Tiger Reserve and the adjoining elephant habitat. Only these bulls, by moving across the flimsy corridors which are disintegrating and shrinking by the day, make Rajaji National Park and Corbett Tiger Reserve a continuous elephant habitat.

Not long ago, the elephant habitat in the former state of Uttar Pradesh was continuous from Katerniaghat in Bahraich Forest Division in the east to river Yamuna in the Shivalik Forest Division in the west. Over the decades, as more and more land came to be occupied by the growing human population, this contiguity was broken. Now there are five isolated elephant populations. The major population of elephants in this tract—about 800-1000—occurs in the Rajaji-Corbett Elephant Range. This is a range of about 5000 km², from the Kathgodam-Haldwani-Lalkuan road in the east to the river Yamuna in the west. This forest tract includes the present day Shivalik and Dehra Dun Forest Divisions, the Rajaji National Park, Corbett Tiger Reserve, parts of Lansdowne Division and Haridwar, Bijnor, Kalagarh, Ramnagar, West Terai and Central Terai Divisions.

The large Rajaji-Corbett population and its habitat has already been broken into three isolated areas because of two major developmental projects. This includes the fourteen kilometre-long Kunaun-Chilla power channel, which was constructed on the eastern bank of the River Ganga in the early 1970s. Around the time the channel was built, there were developmental projects on the west bank of the Ganga, such as the establishment of the Hindustan Antibiotics factory, Raiwala army camp, and the settlement of evacuees from the submersion area of Tehri dam. As a result, the Chilla-Motichur corridor is now unfit for elephant herds to move between Chilla and Motichur across the Ganga.

What has further restricted the movement of elephants between Rajaji and Corbett is the Kotdwar-Lansdowne road, which runs across the narrow Rajaji-Corbett corridor parallel to the River Khoh. The construction of this road has resulted in steep edges and the building of walls, which impede crossing by elephants. Fortunately, elephant bulls still migrate across the power channel and the road, thereby bringing about genetic exchange between otherwise isolated populations. This genetic exchange cannot continue for long if the fragile habitat continuity between these areas is not immediately strengthened by consolidating the corridors.

One summer evening in 1990, as dusk was gathering, Wesley Sunderraj, a researcher from the Wildlife Institute of India, was returning to Kotdwar walking along the Khoh River. He spotted an elephant bull, a tusker, coming along a valley from the direction of the Rajaji National Park towards the Khoh river. Wesley photographed the bull and stayed by the river to see if the bull would cross it. By the time the bull came close to the river it became so dark that Wesley had to abandon his post. He, however, went back to the same area early the next morning, and picked up the trail of the tusker. The elephant had crossed the river and the Kotdwar-Lansdowne road, and walked in the direction of the Corbett Tiger Reserve.

This was the only bull that Wesley had seen using the corridor during the two-year period that he studied the elephant corridor between Rajaji and Corbett. The corridor is to the west of the Khoh. He discovered that there was no movement of cow groups across the corridor because of the steep terrain, which the calves cannot negotiate, and the disturbances caused by people. The cow groups, just to ensure the safety of the calves, avoid areas of disturbances even if they are rich in food resources. Bulls, as they need not care either for the safety of calves or for the group, negotiate even areas of high disturbance in the cover of darkness. Wesley, however, concluded that the growing disturbances in the corridor area—grass, bamboo, fodder and wood collection—may one day stop even the bulls moving across the Rajaji-Corbett corridor. If that happens, the genetic exchange between the populations on the east and west of the Khoh will come to an end forever. The Uttaranchal Government's plan for an express highway between Rajaji and Corbett will make sure that even the occasional movement of elephants ceases.

The number of socially and sexually mature elephant bulls

is an important factor in deciding the genetic virility of elephant populations. Sadly, in many elephant ranges in India, a good example being Periyar Tiger Reserve, uncontrolled poaching of tuskers has drastically depleted the bulls, leading to a disproportionate sex ratio. The adult sex ratio reported in Periyar Tiger Reserve is one male to 120 females. Although there are some tuskless bulls (*makhnas*) in the population, this disproportionate sex ratio has two certain disastrous consequences. One is that a proportion of females may not be able to mate, even though elephant bulls are polygynous. The other is that the cow, which selects the bull, may allow younger bulls to mate with her in the absence of mature bulls. Such mating on a large scale and for several generations, which is bound to happen in a place like Periyar, can eventually have a drastic effect on the quality—size and vigour—of the elephants.

Corbett Tiger Reserve is, fortunately, one of the few places in Asia where tuskers have not yet come within the sights of the poacher's gun. As a result, there is about one adult bull for every three adult cows, and in April 1996, 80 per cent of the cows had either calves or young juveniles. In Periyar, in 1990, only about 30 per cent of the cows were reported to be accompanied by young.

When a cow comes into oestrus, several bulls compete for her and only the best bull—sexually and socially mature, fully grown, virile and aggressive—in that locality is able to mate with the female, and thereby pass on the best genes to the population. This biological phenomenon warrants continued protection to elephant bulls. When the bull is around twenty years old, he begins to experience a condition known as *musth*. The phenomenon of musth was first described in captive Asian elephants, and though physiologically well explained, its role in the ecology of elephants was not understood for a long time. The period of musth may last from a few days to more than three months, depending on the age of the animal and its body condition. The body condition of bulls coming into musth is usually very good. Studies have shown that during musth, the level of the male hormone testosterone goes up and bulls usually range far and wide in search of females in oestrus. Some researchers have compared musth with rutting in other ungulates. Musth bulls are usually very aggressive towards other bulls, and guard oestrous females vigorously. Bulls not in musth are also known to mate successfully, but the urge to search for females in oestrus is very strong in musth males.

One morning in Dhikala, driving to the chaur, we saw a twenty-five-year-old bull standing nervously at the edge of a forest. We stopped the vehicle and watched him. After a minute or so, he started running into the chaur. The reason became apparent when we saw another bull with thick short tusks, about thirty to thirty-five years old, in musth. He was walking threateningly from the forest edge towards the younger bull, which beat a hasty retreat from the area into the chaur. When we followed the musth bull, we found him courting a female.

The vegetation mostly hid the other members of the group. A little later, we heard loud vocalisation in the form of rumblings and squeals and trumpets. We grabbed our binoculars and started to scan the group. The musth male had mounted the female and was mating with her. After about forty seconds, he dismounted and we could again hear excited vocalisations. We hurried to the group and took a good look at the musth male. He was in excellent physical condition. He kept very close to the female and guarded her through the three days we watched him. During our observations, we saw the musth bull chasing away at least eight different adult bulls of varying ages from his vicinity.

One evening in December 1991, we were on the trail of a large radio-collared bull elephant in the Chilla part of Rajaji National Park. He was a massive animal, over ten feet high, probably over five tons heavy. We fondly called that 46-year-old bull 'Big Boss'. When we finally tracked him down, he was with a cow group, vigorously courting a female. Musth profusely flowed down both his cheeks. A cow elephant comes into oestrus only for two or three days in a year, and if she conceives, she may not be in oestrus again for two or three years. This means that very few cows are in oestrus at a given time. Researchers have always wondered how adult bulls, especially ones in musth, find females in oestrus. Catherine Payne and her colleagues, while working on infrasound communication by elephants in Etosha National Park in Namibia, discovered that females in oestrus give a peculiar call, inaudible to humans. They have speculated that elephant bulls hear this, and are able to home in on females in oestrus. During the three to four month period that Big Boss was in musth, he wandered over an area of about 200 kms² and during this period we located him with eight different female groups. What he was doing was obvious— roaming through his home range looking for receptive females. By the time the winter cool had given way to summer heat, his body condition declined, he lost his urge for sex, and became solitary.

Justus Joshua, a researcher from the Wildlife Institute of India, then studying elephants in Rajaji, observed a great contraction in the home range of Big Boss—from 200 kms² in winter to about 20 kms² in summer. His behaviour was transformed as well. In summer, Big Boss spent the whole day resting in a cool valley far away from any form of human disturbance. He stirred out of his hide only after darkness had descended. Thereafter, he went to a small water hole dug out by gujjars in the dry riverbed, and drank his fill. This took almost an hour. He also threw water on his body several times to cool off. Thereafter he disappeared into the forest to feed, largely on the bark and branches of the trees, which he pushed down effortlessly.

Early one morning, when Justus tracked down Big Boss, the bull was still feeding, and there was a cow group with him. Interestingly, when Big Boss stripped the bark from a tree and pushed it down, the entire group gathered around and started feeding on the tree, leaving very little space for Big Boss. This made him move away and find another tree to similarly 'debark' and push down. Perhaps to the consternation of Big Boss, even this tree was taken over by the group. It occurred to Justus that one of the reasons for Big Boss leading a solitary life in summer (the major reason was lack of sexual desire) could be to avoid competition with cow groups over food trees, which are hard to come by in a degraded and heavily disturbed habitat like Chilla.

On quantifying debarking by elephants in Rajaji and Corbett, we found debarking begins in winter, and reaches its peak in summer. Summer in most elephant ranges is characterised by lack of forage and water. This is also the time when the elephants suffer from a lack of calcium in their diet. This makes them debark and feed on cambium, the internal tissue of the bark, along which plant sap, rich in calcium, flows from the root system to the canopy. Interestingly, debarking is much more common in Rajaji than in Corbett. We attribute this to the immense biotic pressures, like wood cutting, lopping and cattle grazing, which have led to severe degradation of the habitat in most places. The area around Dhikala does not have much incidence of debarking because of the rich forage that the Ramganga valley offers even in summer. The streams, rivers and the soil around Dhikala may be richer in calcium than in Rajaji. This, however, needs to be studied.

In November 1995, the fifty-year-old Big Boss came into musth and followed a young female who was in oestrus and in the company of a large herd. According to the wildlife guards, the herd had about sixty elephants including three or four bulls. As Big Boss courted a female, one young bull in his prime, maybe about thirty-five years old, with dagger-like tusks, attacked him. The fight raged over the riverbeds and hills, through forests and open areas. The guards tried to disperse the bulls by firing in the air, but their efforts were in vain. Big Boss fought valiantly but the fight was uneven. Big Boss's energy reserves were low because of his age, and exhausted by the long battle, he slipped and fell into a narrow *nallah* from which he could not get up. This made him hopelessly vulnerable, and exploiting his hapless situation, the young bull gored him to death. Thus ended the life of a magnificent and noble bull who strolled through the Chilla forests in all his majesty for more than two decades. He had allowed us to approach him very close on several occasions and neither charged nor chased us. We mourned his death like a friend's.

The elephant bulls of Corbett Tiger Reserve and the adjoining areas are a peerless asset, which need to be assiduously protected for ecological and aesthetic reasons. The sight of magnificent bulls, strolling across the Dhikala and Paterpani chaurs, giving the impression that they are lords of the Reserve and afraid of none, can thrill any visitor. Their trumpet calls and fights, both mock and real, can return us to a primordial world, when woolly mammoths roamed the land, and man was hunter and as well as prey.

Much needs to be done to ensure the future of these bulls. Effective protection should be continued. Corridors across the Ganga and Khoh rivers should be strengthened, so that the bulls can continue to pass on genes from one population to the other. This vast stretch of prime elephant and tiger habitat should be freed of human disturbances, as much as possible, to benefit all forms of wildlife.

Before 1993, gujjar buffaloes roamed the banks of River Palain in Halduparao range, in the present-day Corbett Reserve. Their presence made large wild mammals shy away. The immense wildlife potential of the area was realised by A. S. Negi, former Director of Corbett Tiger Reserve. In February 1993, he persuaded the gujjars to move to another area, freeing Halduparao of cattle and humans. The results were remarkable. When we visited Halduparao in May 1995, a herd of elephants trailed by a massive bull was feeding peacefully. There was a number of sambar in the nearby Mandolti *sot*, which was once an abode of buffaloes. Tiger signs were numerous in the *sot*. Such far-sighted conservation measures need to be taken all over the Rajaji-Corbett elephant range, where human disturbance is destroying critical wildlife habitats. Fortunately, several conservation agencies like the newly formed 'Operation Eye of the Tiger' and 'Corbett Foundation' are willing to work with the Forest Department to help solve the problems of the Reserve.

A menacing postcript

The major mortality factor for the elephant bulls of Rajaji-Corbett till recently was death from fights between adult bulls over females in oestrous. However, in December 2000 and January-February 2001, eight tuskers in the core area of Corbett Tiger Reserve were killed by poachers. This was completely unexpected. We were under the impression that Corbett Tiger Reserve, the premier protected area in the country, is a well-guarded reserve.

Post-mortem reports showed that at least three bulls were killed by arrows with chisel-type iron arrowheads. Such arrows can penetrate the thick skin of an elephant only when they are shot with a powerful tool like a cross-bow. Other evidence such as the wrapping of cotton thread on the bamboo shaft at the base of the arrow-head and broken balloons (presumably the balloons were used to carry the poison) indicate the possible role of Lisu tribals from Arunachal Pradesh. Lisus reportedly have such traditions of making poisoned arrows. The poison is probably extracted from the tuber of *Aconitum balfourii,* a high altitude plant. The *modus operandi* is to shoot the elephant with poison arrows, and follow it till it goes down, which takes four to six hours. The enormous amount of blood flowing from the dead elephants indicated that the poachers cut off the trunk of the unfortunate bulls at its base, to remove the tusks, possibly even when it was alive. Since an elephant bull takes so many hours to go down, and has to be very closely followed during this period, this form of poaching can be done only in undisturbed core areas, which are seldom visited by people. The wildlife staff too rarely patrols core areas, perhaps unrealistically thinking these areas are off bounds even for poachers.

In May 2001 and in April 2002, spending three days each time, I counted nearly a hundred elephants in Dhikala and Paterpani chaurs, and could sex and age about ninety of them. I did not see a single big tusker. Does this mean that the poachers have removed most of the tuskers from the Reserve, and we got an inkling of the magnitude of the poaching problem only in December 2000 and January 2001? If the poachers have killed most of the big tuskers, then it will mean two decades of rigorous anti-poaching efforts to give room and time to young calves to grow into majestic bulls that stroll the Dhikala and Paterpani chaurs again.

8   Revisiting Corbett Country

Kanda

The glow of electric light spilled out from Dhikala, the main tourist centre in the Ramganga valley. Light from distant villages twinkled along the long mountain ridge beyond the Mandal river. None of these lights existed when Jim Corbett stayed in the Kanda forest bungalow, in pursuit of the Kanda maneater. Standing at an altitude of 1035 metres, the bungalow has the Ramganga Valley to its south, and the mountain ridge to its north. The century-old house has not been altered since Corbett stayed there in May 1933. Sitting in the cool shade of a banyan tree in fruit, I discussed the forests around the bungalow with A. S. Negi of the Indian Forest Service. It was 1998.

One remarkable difference in the area between Corbett's time and now, is the near absence of Kanda village, which had fifteen odd houses and was situated about 200 metres northeast of the bungalow. A large lantana patch and a giant semul tree now mark the land where the village stood. The village has returned to wilderness but for an ugly two-storeyed yellow mansion. Why has the village vanished?

In the past most villages in the lower reaches of the Outer Himalaya had two settlements, one for winter and the other for summer, three to five kilometres from the winter settlement up in the hills. The summer settlement was always situated near a perennial source of water. In early April most of the populace with their livestock moved to the summer settlement, where rain-fed crops such as ragi (*Eleusine coracana*) were grown, and the cattle was grazed on the nearby hills. Kanda village was abandoned when, in the early 1970s, people started living permanently in Kanda *nallah,* their winter settlement, on the right bank of the Mandal river. Summer villages have been similarly abandoned in many places in the Himalaya, and one major reason for this is the drying up of water sources with habitat degradation, caused by excessive lopping, fire and grazing.

When the Kanda maneater appeared on the present day northern boundary of Corbett Tiger Reserve, the inhabitants of Painaun, Bungi and Bickla Badalpur begged Corbett to rescue them. Corbett found the request irresistible, and arrived in Kanda in May 1933. After climbing innumerable miles up and down steep hills with scree for several days, to make contact with the wary maneater, he finally came across the pugmarks of the tiger at the edge of a ploughed field overlooking a village. From his descriptions, the village seems to be Taria, which is about seven kilometres northwest of the forest bungalow. While circling around the village looking for tiger signs, Corbett killed a four metre-long king cobra with stones. This gave him a feeling of great satisfaction: he had a deep-rooted conviction that however much he might try, all his efforts to kill a maneater would be pointless unless preceded by the killing of a snake. He finally shot the Kanda maneater in the uncertain light of early morning, after a night-long vigil up in a tree. Interestingly, talking about the Kanda maneater, Corbett does not mention any other tiger in the area; the only other wildlife he mentions, besides the cobra, is a group of langur.

The slopes that are south of Kanda, eventually leading to the Ramganga valley, are richer in wildlife than the northern slopes. They are covered with a dense growth of sal and an understorey dominated by *Clerodendron infortunatum* and *Ardisia solanacea*. One evening, we decided to explore the southern slopes. We left Kanda at five p.m., and first went to the spring amidst giant mango trees in the valley between Kanda village and the bungalow. The spring, which looked like a small shallow well with cold clear water, was covered with stone slabs on three sides and on the top. This spring is reported to be the only water source within a radius of about three kilometres from Kanda. In the past, the spring provided drinking water to the summer population of Kanda village and to the wildlife of the area. Now, only the staff of the Forest Department and the ten men who stay in the bungalow use it. The staff frequently see sambar, barking deer, langur and rhesus monkeys drinking at the spring. We saw leopard tracks. The spring could be an excellent place to record how often tigers drink from this source of water, from the tracks in the wet mud around it.

We drove along the road down the slope till Hathi Pani, a spring four kilometres from Kanda, carefully looking for goral in the steep terrain on either side of the road. We saw only four groups of langur, but near the spring, with the fourth group of langur, we saw a small group of chital. By the end of the drive we were at Phulai chaur (grassland) on the right bank of the Ramganga. As we reached the valley, we saw our first sambar (an adult doe with a yearling female) and several groups of chital. We drove across the chaur and through the jamun grove to Ringora (the name comes from the ringal bamboo *Arundinaria falcata*, which possibly occurred there). There were many groups of chital but we saw neither tiger nor elephant, which was surprising. When nightjars began to call, we drove back to Kanda.

Teria and Pand

Our plan for the next day was to drive to Teria *kaul* and walk to Lohachaur, visiting Teria and Pand villages on the way, a distance of about ten kilometres. We walked through sal forest to Teria. The path went along a fire line. A kilometre from the village, we saw a Devi temple, and were later told by the villagers that the place where Corbett shot the Teria maneater was to the north of the temple. On the outskirts of the village, we met Mohanand Dhyani, sixty-four years old, who accompanied us to the village. We asked him if he had known Corbett. He replied that his paternal uncle had been one of the victims of the maneater of Teria. He took us to Mahesha Nanda, 103 years old, who, he said, would perhaps be able to tell us more about Corbett. Mahesha was small and bent with age, yet he was sweeping the veranda of his small house when we entered. He was hard of hearing, and people said his memory was unreliable. We asked him some questions but could not get much out of him about the past.

Teria village had a population of about forty families, who made a living by cultivating the land and performing religious rituals for the Rajputs of nearby villages. They complained that crop raiding by sambar and wild pigs was a serious problem, and they would happily move out of the jungle provided they are given a suitable resettlement package. The presence of villages like Teria in a place like Corbett Tiger Reserve has one definite advantage: it provides the labour force vital for road and fire management. Nevertheless, it also causes immense damage to habitat and disturbs wildlife.

We left Teria at seven a.m. and after walking a kilometre or so through sal forest, we entered a well-wooded cool valley, where the sun lit the ground in patches. This forest was alive with birds such as black bulbul, White-crested Laughing Thrush, beautiful niltava, White-throated Laughing Thrush, Rusty-cheeked Scimitar Babbler and Khaleej Pheasant. As we reached Pand village, we heard repeated alarm calls of sambar and barking deer from Nagron *sot*, which eventually joins Lohachaur, a good tiger area in Corbett Tiger Reserve. On the outskirts of Pand village, we saw several abandoned terraced fields, overgrown with sixty to eighty year old sal trees. Pand village, with much larger terraced fields and better soil, looked much more prosperous than Teria. Of the thirty families that originally lived there, about fifteen had moved out of the village. The rest, since they were also cultivating the land of those who had left the village, gave the impression that they led a contented life, and had no desire to move out of the village.

As we descended from Pand, we went past a Kali temple under a five-hundred year old banyan tree. Under the tree was the stone statue of a goddess seated on an exceptionally long tiger. The final descent to Lohachaur was steep, through dense jungle. We realised that during our walk through the Reserve, although we tried to be as silent as possible, we had seen only two groups of wild boar, a barking deer, a common langur group and a tiger pug mark.

A day later, at the Ramganga Corbett Fishing Lodge at Marchula, we sat by the river discussing conservation problems in this part of Corbett Tiger Reserve. We learnt that during the past six months, at least six tigers had been poisoned around Durga Devi temple. But the tigers had neither been skinned, nor had their bones been removed; we concluded that the poisoning was in retaliation to cattle killings, and was not the handiwork of poachers. As for wild prey for the tiger, the manager said that sambar were rare, and once he had seen two domestic dogs killing a sambar near the river in front of the lodge.

Mohan

We were sure that the reason for tigers getting poisoned was the lack of sufficient wild ungulate prey, which forced tigers to kill livestock and earned them the wrath of the people. We decided to drive to Kart Kanoula, sixteen kilometres from the lodge at an altitude of 1220 metres, to count sambar and other ungulates along the road. Kart Kanoula is the village in the vicinity of which the Mohan maneater took up its quarters before Corbett shot it.

We left the lodge well before sunrise. We drove slowly, looking for animals, and the habitat on both the sides of the road looked suitable for sambar, barking deer and goral. In places where we had an extensive view of the area, either up in the hills or down in the valley, we stopped, got out of the vehicle and scanned the forests with binoculars. Along the sixteen-kilometre drive, we saw just one barking deer and heard another. Even langur were not visible.

Reaching the foresters' hut in Kart Kanoula, where Corbett had stayed nearly sixty-five years earlier, involves a climb of fifteen minutes from the road. As we walked up, black partridges called all around the village, and groups of Streaked Laughing Thrushes skulked through the understorey. In Corbett's time, the hut was ten feet square, with two small rooms, one used as a kitchen and the other as the fuel store. Now, though dilapidated, the hut has a large hall with a wooden floor, wooden walls and a tin roof.

Kart Kanoula is on the ridge separating the Kosi and Ramganga watersheds. The north-facing slope of the ridge had terraced cultivation with oak (*Quercus incana*) and pine (*Pinus roxburghiana*). On the south there was a patch of disturbed sal forest, which extended down for a kilometre. Further down, there was dense vegetation, continuous with Corbett Tiger Reserve on the west and the forests west and east of the Kosi river. Clearly visible from our hut was Mohan village, which has not changed much over the decades, and the forest bungalow where Corbett stayed before embarking on a four-thousand feet chase after a tiger on a blistering hot day in May.

The 'road' along which Corbett walked to the hut still exists, and is used by children who come to a small school built on the ridge near the hut. When Corbett had enquired about the Mohan maneater, the villagers had said that they always knew when the tiger came into the village by the low moaning sound it made. Corbett correctly concluded that the tiger was suffering from a wound and since the tiger only felt it when it was in motion, the wound was probably on one of its legs. The villagers were not convinced. They were sure no sportsman had wounded the tiger. When the tiger was shot, they found that the sole of its left foreleg was skewered with about thirty porcupine quills. The villagers concluded that Corbett was gifted with second sight.

When Corbett came to shoot the Mohan maneater, he walked 38 kilometres from Ramnagar to Kart Kanoula. On the first night, as he did not have permission to occupy the Gargia Forest Bungalow, he slept near the Kosi river in the open. At night, he heard what he thought were stones falling off the cliff onto the rocks below on the far side of the Kosi river. When he investigated later, he found that the sound was being made by a colony of frogs in a marsh by the road!

The area along which Corbett walked then, is transformed. Between the Kosi River and the Gargia Forest bungalow, there is the Corbett Riverside Resort, which has destroyed the marsh. There are encroachments, resorts and villages for a distance of about ten kilometres between Mohan and Bijrani, disrupting the wildlife habitat. In several places, exotic teak plantations have replaced the natural vegetation, impoverishing the wildlife habitat.

Talla Des, Chuka and Thak

Our next destination, on our way to the terrain of the Talla Des maneater, was Tanakpur. The drive from Ramnagar to

Tanakpur went across the fertile terai habitat. Had we done this journey five hundred years ago (on elephant back perhaps) we would have travelled through impenetrable elephant grass, across marshes. We would have seen herds of elephants, rhinos, buffaloes, swamp deer and hog deer, and would have flushed numerous Bengal floricans and tigers. Hundreds of marsh crocodiles would have plunged into water bodies on seeing us. Now, as we drove along, there was paddy being planted, wheat being harvested, and sugar cane. With sunflowers in bloom, the fields looked from a distance as if they had a sprinkling of gold. Besides, there were mango orchards, poplar, *Eucalyptus* and teak plantations. Every inch of land was intensively cultivated. We crossed numerous rivers with clear water (free from factory waste), with patches of the reed *Typha elephantina*. The roads were broad and well paved in most places, and therefore our driver raced along at great speed, overtaking numerous tractors and trucks carrying off the produce of the land. The hot sun and the warm breeze coming from the fields made us drowsy.

Tanakpur, now a sprawling town, is on the right bank of the Sharda, and our host in Tanakpur was J.S. Rawat, whose house is right on the bank of the river. Mr Rawat was a well-respected social worker, involved with the 'Save Mahseer' programme for the Sharda and Ladiya rivers that the National Bureau of Fish Genetic Resources, Lucknow initiated. About seventy years old, he had as a boy listened to sounds of an epic battle between a bull tusker and two tigers that raged all through the night close to his house. The next day, the village gathered around the dead elephant. The battle is epitomised in the *Journal of the Bombay Natural History Society* (Vol. 41) by E.A. Smythies. Mr Rawat said that until ten years ago, his family could hear tigers calling at night from the Nepal jungles across the Sharda.

Koels, crows and magpie-robins heralded the day, as we got ready to make our long journey to Talla Kote, where Corbett shot the Talla Des maneater in April 1929. Our plan was to drive to Selagarh, walk from Selagarh to Sem via Kot Kendri, Thak and Chuka, fish in the Ladiya-Sharda confluence, halt at Sem for the night, and climb the mountain the next day, to reach Talla Kote. Our worry was the heat, which could make our climb up the mountain extremely difficult.

The distance between Tanakpur and Selagarh is 21 kilometres, and the habitat on both sides of the road looked intact, good enough for sambar and barking deer. But we saw only pilgrims and rhesus macaques on the road. The first hour from Selagarh was a steep and difficult climb, and then for about twenty minutes, the climb went largely through densely wooded forest, where there were trees like *Prunus* persica, *P. cerasoides* and *Bassia buteracea*.

Somewhere on this steep path, in the winter of 1936, the Chuka maneater sprang upon a man who was carrying a sack of jaggery, half of which was on his head, the other half on his back. The tiger's teeth got caught in the sack, and he carried it away down the hillside, without causing the man any injury. We, however, saw very little wildlife: sambar tracks at a natural salt lick, and a goral, which hurried down a steep slope.

We spent an hour in Kot Kendri, a village owned by the people of Chuka, and here we met Jeet Singh, an uncle of Dungar Singh, whose mother had been the last victim of the Talla Des maneater. The habitat around Kot Kendri appeared overused and degraded, and the villagers were harvesting the local variety of wheat.

The Chuka maneater was shot by Corbett in April 1937 in the Ladiya valley, below Kot Kendri. The Ladiya-Sharda confluence was visible from the village. The river Ladiya had clear bluish water, and the Sharda, a snow-fed river, had lime-white water. We could also see the path from Sem to Tamlia, which went vertically up a mountain face. This sent a shiver down my spine, as we had to take that very path the next day, in the hot May sun. Even Corbett and his team, with the April sun blazing down on their backs, and without a single tree to shade them, had found that climb the steepest and most exhausting he and his men had ever undertaken.

From Kot Kendri, the path to Thak went over a pine-covered ridge, where we saw some goral pellets. Before the climb, we sat in the cool shade of the deep valley and had a late breakfast of bread, bananas and eggs. The valley had only a trickle of water. Beyond the ridge, the path went across abandoned terraced fields. Although there were patches of rain clouds overhead, which gave some relief from the heat, the walk to Thak was exhausting. The forests on either side of the path appeared ideal for sambar and barking deer, but except for pellets of barking deer, we saw no sign of these animals. Corbett's descriptions indicate that these animals were very common in his time.

Thak village came into prominence in 1937 when two human beings and two cows were slaughtered on the same day by the maneater in the vicinity of the village. By the winter of 1938, the village was deserted, since it had become the favoured abode of the Thak maneater. A man who said that his was the only family still living in Thak, accompanied us there from Kot Kendri. All other families, he said, had settled around Selagarh as priests, and the income from the devotees who thronged the Purnagiri temple was so good that the priests could afford their own shops and taxis. We knew that there were no more man-eating tigers around Thak. Yet the walk through the deserted village where the yards were overgrown with nettle and other weeds, gave us the uneasy feeling that we could be ambushed by a maneater any time.

The early afternoon was still hot, and we stopped in the shade of a giant mango tree to drink water from the spring that arises from the base of the tree. I had been there before, five years earlier, on Corbett's trail. Corbett describes this tree and the spring when writing about the Thak maneater. We were saddened to see that the old tree had lost two thirds of its canopy to heavy winds, and its main trunk had been badly burnt. It was clear that its glorious days were over. Even the spring, which people did not use much, was shallow and covered with rotting leaf litter. We cleared the spring, allowed clean water to accumulate, drank the water and selected a place clear of weeds to lie down for a nap. Nearby, there were signs that people had camped and cooked under the tree. The house of the only family in the village was about 200 metres away.

As we slept, rain clouds gathered, and thunder and lightning woke us. There were a few raindrops, which forced us to hurry down the valley to Chuka, about four kilometres away. Initially the path went through abandoned agricultural fields, and then largely through dense jungle dominated by sal. Soon there was a tremendous hailstorm followed by an hour-long drizzle. We took shelter at the house of Ummed Singh, who had helped me so much on my earlier trip to Chuka in 1993.

The rain brought the temperature down substantially, and mist drifted over the mountains which had radiated intense heat a few hours ago. But now our plans for fishing had gone haywire. The turbulent Ladiya and Sharda carried debris and logs. Yet we fished at the confluence for an hour, hoping to hook a mahseer. The confluence, which in one day had yielded enough to feed Corbett's camp of thirty men in April 1937, did not offer us a single fish—as when I had tried my luck there five years earlier. At least some things had not changed!

In the rapidly fading light, we walked to Sem; two forest watchers had gone ahead of us to find a place for us to stay the night and cook our supper. Even now, Sem is a hamlet of about ten houses, as it was in September 1938, when the Thak maneater killed the mother of the headman within a yard of her hut. We stayed in the house of Madhav Singh, who said he had bought the hut and the land from the childless headman. He showed us where the hut had previously stood, at the end of the village near the river.

We left Sem when it was still dark. The path went along a jeepable road till village Khet. The Sharda flowed peacefully on our right, and on either side of the road, multitudes of birds began their morning activities. Beyond Khet, there was a wide riverbed which joined the Sharda. We looked for signs of large mammals on the sandy riverbed but saw only a Spur-winged Plover. We took the only path that goes up the mountain from the dry riverbed and after fifty metres or so, the path branched in three directions. The middle path, which Corbett may have taken, went along a narrow valley, towards the ridge. We took the path to the left, hoping to rejoin the middle path somewhere up in the mountain. The leaf litter was soft, and the ground wet and yielding. It was cloudy, with the occasional drizzle, thunder and lightning. We forged ahead steadily. On the way, we flushed three goral: the young in the group bleated like a goat-kid and all three raced down a steep slope. Otherwise there was very little evidence of wildlife, and the trail was littered with cow dung all along. When Corbett climbed the mountain, there was only one inhabited place on its southern face, a hamlet of two huts; now there were many concrete houses.

We stopped to have our breakfast, and realised that we had no more water to drink. The climb seemed interminable, and the mountain looming over and ahead insurmountable. As we sat discussing whether we had taken the wrong path, we heard cattle bells up in the mountain, a little to our right. This gave us the hope that we might find some water. Dark rain clouds, occasional thunder, and lightning indicated an impending storm. With some worry and renewed vigour, we went ahead. Soon we passed buffaloes feeding near an abandoned settlement which had no water. We crossed a deep *nallah* that had water polluted with buffalo dung and urine. As we stopped near a house to enquire about the availability of water, the storm broke out. Hurriedly, we sought permission from the man of the house, Nath Singh, and took shelter in the house. The storm raged for about three hours, which gave us enough time to talk to Nath Singh, cook, eat lunch and have a nap.

Nath Singh, seventy-two years old, said that his house, the oldest on the southern slope, had been built a hundred years ago. We wondered whether this was the place Corbett had stayed at, and whether the spring nearby was the one in which Corbett had had his bath before leaving for Talla Kote, where he first made contact with the Talla Des maneater. Soon after the rains, there was brilliant sunshine, and the green leaves washed of dust glistened in the bright sun. When we came onto the track up which Corbett and his party had laboured nearly sixty years before, we halted for a spell to admire the view as Corbett had. The Sharda was murky, running almost in a straight line from Khet to its confluence with the Ladiya. Then it disappeared behind the Nepal hills and reappeared closer to Kaladhunga. Chuka, Tanakpur, and the river beyond Tanakpur were not visible. The rains had given a tinge of blue to the ridge where Thak and Kot Kendri were situated.

We climbed ahead along the path. The last twenty-five minutes of the climb to the top of the ridge was difficult, and went past several large oak and mango trees. *Woodfordia fruticosa* bushes, with their crimson red flowers, lit up the forest. A Yellow-cheeked Tit rummaged in the canopy of an oak tree for insects. On top of the ridge there was a Dhankaji temple. Strong winds howled through the nearby deodar and chir pine trees.

Sixty years before, when Corbett reached the top, there was a six-foot wide forest road going east to west along the top of the ridge. Here he was faced with a dilemma, for there were no villages in sight and he did not know in which direction to go. Eventually he left a sign on the road to enable his men to follow him, and walked east. In that early April so many years ago, Nature was at its best: deciduous trees were putting out new leaves, each of a different shade of green or bronze; flowers were competing with one another, and the birds were on their nesting grounds, their joyous mating songs echoing around. On the forest road, besides the numerous marks of the tiger there were many tracks of leopard, sambar, bear, barking deer and pigs. After walking on the road for about an hour, Corbett came to a village, learnt it was Tamali, and that the village, Talla Kote, where the tiger had got its last victim, was somewhere in the west. He walked back to the place where he had left the sign for his men, changed the sign to indicate that he was going west and then walked along the forest road. The road ran through a forest of giant oak trees standing knee-deep in bracken and maidenhair fern. After walking about eight kilometres, Corbett crossed a crystal-clear stream, and then reached Talla Kote. He shot the two grown-up cubs of the maneater, and injured the maneater before sunset. How he pursued and eventually killed the maneater, when he was suffering from an injury to his left eardrum which made him partly deaf, is graphically described in Corbett's story of the Talla Des maneater.

On reaching the top, we were not in the dilemma that Corbett was. The six-foot wide road was there, but now neither tiger nor sambar would have walked along it. There was a prosperous village hardly a hundred metres from the road, and the magnificent oak forests have been replaced with degraded scrub.

We saw relics of those fine oak forests on top of the two

hills about five kilometres to the west. Nath Singh had suggested that we walk through the village to reach the road to Tamali. Late in the evening we entered the pine-oak forest, from which arose the crystal-clear stream which Corbett must have crossed. One fork of the stream descended into the valley in the form of a waterfall over a steep rock face about fifteen metres high, covered with lush green bushes. Water flowed through the bushes like molten silver. Light in the forest was diffuse; the red flowers of the numerous *Woodfordia fruticosa* bushes, and the lush green grass sprouting in patches, added colour to the hill slope, which was covered with gold-rust pine needles. The only mammal we saw in the forest was a group of rhesus macaques. Cattle bells rang ahead of us somewhere in the forest, and the steady sound of the flourmill came from the village below. The valley ahead of us, with numerous human settlements, had no room left either for sambar or for tiger. We had come across sambar signs only between Teria and Pand, and between Selagarh and the ridge on the way to Kot Kendri. We saw tiger tracks only near Pand. Our brief survey of Corbett's maneating tigers' range had come to an end, and it was time for us to return home to think, and plan what could be done to restore the wildlife abundance of this range.

Jim Corbett's maneating tigers' range sprawled from Kanda in the west to Chuka in the east, and from Mukteswar and Champawat in the north to Thak in the south. His accounts clearly show that even in those days, tigers were scarce in the hills. Tigers other than maneaters were shot only in the Chowgarh hills and in Talla Des. Corbett's accounts of the maneating tigers of Mukteswar, Kanda, Champawat and Mohan do not mention any other tigers. Interestingly, even now tigers are rare in Kanda, which, as the crow flies, is hardly ten kilometres from the Ramganga valley, the prime tiger habitat in the Corbett Tiger Reserve. Among the 350 entries by visitors in the Kanda forest bungalow visitor's book from 1973 to 1997, there is only one mention of a tiger. The reasons for the rarity of tigers in a place like Kanda which is situated in the outer Himalaya, could be the nature of the terrain, where water is scarce for about six months (January to June), and the dominance of unpalatable species like sal, *Clerodendron infortunatum* and *Ardisia solanacea*. Both factors discourage the sambar, the tiger's preferred prey.

The Talla Des maneater raised two cubs to adulthood in spite of her injury, and this we can attribute to the excellent oak forests, still found in Talla Des, able to support a high density of sambar, wild pig, barking deer and langur. It is worthy noting that the tigress, through eight years, killed a hundred and fifty people, who would have contributed only partly to her diet. Talla Des was possibly one of the few places in the Kumaon Himalaya where tigers were successfully breeding in the hills.

From our journey in the tracks of Corbett's kills, it is apparent that over the decades the status of tiger and its prey species has declined dramatically all over Corbett's range, as has happened in the entire range of the tiger. Tigers, for example, no longer breed in the Ladiya valley, as when the Chuka maneater operated.

Can we bring the tiger back into Corbett's range? Land use practices, human and livestock population, and poaching, which have eliminated sambar in most places, makes this extremely difficult in the hills. It may be much easier to return the tiger to the forests between Haldwani and the Sharda, where the habitat is much more productive. The immediate task is to control the poaching of wild ungulates, always easier said than done. Many poachers have been eking out a living selling wild meat. Farmers living in and around wildlife habitats have been killing wild ungulates for the pot, and it will be extremely difficult to stop them. During our trip, we were told about tourists shooting leopards and other animals in the Kumaon Himalaya, facilitated by local tour operators.

Corbett Tiger Reserve, which has the only viable population of tigers in the entire range needs special management inputs to enhance prey abundance. The southern boundary forests of the Reserve, which cover an area of about 300 kms², needs the most immediate attention. Two to three hundred firewood cutters, who come on bicycles every day and collect firewood for sale in far-off places, heavily disturb this area. The wildlife guards do not perceive firewood collection as a form of disturbance, and are more concerned about controlling animal poaching. Monoculture plantations, particularly teak, when compared with the surrounding natural vegetation, are inferior habitats for sambar and pig; they do not offer the shade critically needed in summer. Besides, teak plantations do not provide enough cover from December to June to the tiger, a stalking predator, for it to hunt successfully. Therefore the chital and nilgai that are found in the plantations remain largely unavailable to the tiger. According to Kunwar Surendrajit Sinh and Kunwar Virendrajit Sinh, heirs of Tejpur State, Bijnor, who have been living for forty years on a farm in Kiratpur, adjacent to the Reserve, no tigers breed any longer in the southern boundary forests.

This situation has to be changed, and can be done if the plantations are converted to polyculture plantations of species such as *Holoptelia integrifolia*, *Pongamia glabra* and *Dalbergia sissoo*. These species are unpalatable to cattle and wild ungulates, and can provide sufficient shade and cover for wild pig and sambar. This would eventually facilitate tigers breeding in this area, and increase dispersal from the Corbett Tiger Reserve. One direction where the dispersal should go is east. To facilitate this, the forests on the right bank of the Kosi river, between Kumaria and Mohan (ca. 6 kilometres), and between the eastern end of the tourist resorts and Bijrani (7 kilometres) need special protection. These forests connect the Reserve and the Ramnagar forests on the left bank of Kosi. The two small factories between Mohan and Kumaria, which are barely functional now, should be relocated as early as possible, to end human disturbance. Three villages: Ringora, between Dhanagarhi and Bijrani; Amdanda, near Ramnagar; and Tedha, west of Ramnagar on the banks of the Kosi, need to be resettled. This will strengthen the habitat connectivity between the Reserve and the Ramnagar forests. At the time of writing, the Ramnagar forests and Terai West and Central forests are connected by the four-kilometre-wide corridor west of the Bhakhra River, called the Nihal–Bhakhra corridor. This narrow corridor needs the greatest protection. The Terai West and Central plantation divisions need to be converted into jungle again, with total protection from encroachment. Efforts should also be made to connect the forests east and west of Haldwani, by a corridor south of Lalkuan. This, however, is going to be extremely challenging.

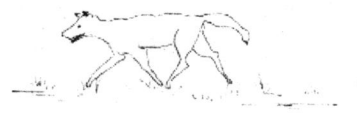

9   The Flight of the Mahseer

In *Maneaters of Kumaon* Corbett describes fishing for mahseer in a river that flowed for some sixty kilometres through a wooded valley teeming with wildlife. As Corbett fished for his dinner, the air was filled with the fragrance of flowers and the spring songs of a multitude of birds. Angling for mahseer in a submontane river in such an atmosphere, Corbett thought, was a sport fit for kings. Long after he had forgotten the weight of the fifty pound fish he had caught, he ruminated, he would remember the beauty of that river valley. Corbett's descriptions fit well with the Ramganga valley in the Corbett Tiger Reserve which is still one of the few strongholds of mahseer in India.

Mahseer is a freshwater, scaly fish that can attain a huge size. In the past mahseer of seventy to eighty kilograms have frequently been caught in Indian waters and it has been reported that the fish can grow to weights exceeding a hundred kilograms.

The etymology of 'mahseer' suggests that the word could mean a fish with 'lion's gameness', 'big scaled fish', 'large headed fish' and 'fish par excellence'. The only other fresh water fish in India comparable to the mahseer in weight is the goonch *Bagarus bagarius* that also thrives in the Ramganga. The mahseer shows more sport for its size than a salmon and therefore is considered the best sportfish in the world. As most mahseer quite avidly take bait such as spoon, plug, fly or live fish, an erroneous impression had gained ground that they are carnivorous and rapacious. But careful studies have shown that they are omnivorous and consume almost anything available in the water, from weeds and snails, to crabs and live fish.

Mahseer inhabit different rivers and reservoirs throughout India, Pakistan, Nepal, Bhutan, Bangladesh, Burma and Sri Lanka. Mahseer experts have recognised six to eight species in India but there is no detailed information on the present status and distribution of these species. The species in Corbett Tiger Reserve is the golden mahseer *Tor putitora* which grows to twenty-five kilograms in the Ramganga river. The different species of mahseer inhabit varied habitats ranging from tropical waters where the temperature in summer goes up to 35°C to sub-Himalayan waters where the winter water temperature drops close to 0°C. Similarly, mahseer occur in streams a few metres above sea level and can also be found in streams at altitudes of 2000 metres.

A.S.T.J. Macdonald says (*Circumventing the Mahseer and*

Other Sporting Fish in India and Burma, 1948) that during floods the mahseer ascends considerable heights to gain the upper reaches of rivers, travelling long distances for fresh feeding grounds and for spawning. They lay their eggs in sheltered rock pools, not in the manner of salmon—all at one time—but a batch of eggs at a time, repeating the process several times through the season. This critical period is when they need the most protection. But unfortunately, over the decades, it is in this vulnerable time that they have been decimated. Fishing methods are varied. People living on the banks of the Ganges, particularly the Dhondar community, have been fishing with line and hook, snares (a long strong fishing line across the river with several nooses tied to it), traps and with throw nets. After the British, anglers fished mahseer with rod and line.

Although accurate data on the catches of mahseer for different parts of the country are not available, comparison of figures from a few isolated surveys as well as observations of anglers and fishery biologists indicate that there is a serious decline in the abundance of mahseer. The traditional methods of fishing are not the decisive factor in the mahseer's decline. It has been dying out from a combination of factors including poisoning, which destroys brood fish and juveniles. Pollution, the silting of rivers and construction of dams have impeded the migration of mahseer, which is crucial for spawning. But most lethal is the use of dynamite, easily available from organisations such as the Public Works Department and Border

Road Organisation. Dynamite kills adults, young fishes, fry and even the developing larvae. It has doomed the mahseer in most parts of its range.

Compared with other commercial fishes, mahseer is more prone to depletion and extinction. One of the prime habitat requirements of mahseers is clean water, that is becoming rarer and rarer in its range. To breed, the fish has to reach its favoured spawning grounds which need to be comparatively calm, with well-oxygenated water and a bed of sand or gravel. The journey to these grounds is often fraught with risks and dangers.

The fecundity of mahseer as compared to other commercially exploited species is also very low. For example the Deccan or khudree mahseer (*Tor khudree*) has a paltry 6000 eggs/kg body weight as compared to 2,61,000 eggs/kg body weight of rohu (*Labeo rohita*) and 1,33,000 eggs/kg body weight of catla (*Catla catla*). The eggs of the mahseer are demersal (capable of sinking in the riverbed) and therefore, if there is mud on the bed instead of sand or gravel, they can sink and perish. The hatching period of khudree mahseer is 60 to 80 hours and of the Golden or Himalayan mahseer 80 to 96 hours compared to 18 hours for catla and rohu. Further, the semiquiescent stage soon after hatching, when fish are vulnerable to all kinds of predation, is three days for catla and rohu and double that for khudree mahseer. The mahseer is therefore altogether more vulnerable to all forms of decimation.

My affair with the mahseer is an old one. One quiet evening a decade ago, alongside the tunnel through which water charges from the Parambikulam reservoir to the Thunakadavu reservoir in Parambikulam Wildlife Sanctuary in Kerala, I sat watching mahseer. The blue-finned mahseer (*Tor khudree*) of Parambikulam is one of the six to eight species of mahseer that occur within Indian limits and one among the three found in southern India. This species once had a much wider distribution, but is now largely confined to Chalakudy and Periyar rivers in Kerala which flow through protected areas.

The descent to the edge of the gorge, through a dense bamboo grove, needed to be done with some caution because of the formidable current. Cold, clean water from the tunnel to the reservoir rushed along the man-made narrow, deep gorge. The tunnel entry was where the larger mahseer (five to ten kilograms) of the reservoir came in groups of twenty to hunt smaller fish. When groups of such large mahseer swam up the mighty current, leaping, splashing and hunting smaller fish which jumped above the water in hundreds, it was like watching crocodiles hunting. In the gathering darkness or early in the morning, when mist rested over the reservoir water, I would sit precariously on the edge of a cold slippery rock and watch the mighty mahseer hunt its fleeing prey. Now in the Parambikulam, as in the Ramganga, the mahseer hunts less and less.

The Ramganga River, where Corbett fished for his dinner

sometime in the early part of this century, has been transformed because of the construction of a dam across the river at Kalagarh in the late 1960s. As a result the water in the reservoir now spreads for about 80 km² soon after the rains in July-August, inundating nearly 16 kilometres of the river from Kalagarh to Dhikala. The 22-kilometre stretch of the river from Domunda, where it enters the National Park, to Dhikala, remains what it was a hundred years ago, with abundant wildlife on both banks. Mahseer fishing in the Reserve is permitted in the Ramganga river upstream of Domunda, in the Mandal river draining the Mandal valley north of Kanda and in the Kosi river upstream of Kumaria. All these fishing sites are in the buffer zone of the Reserve. The most important rivers in the Reserve where mahseer spawn are Ramganga, Mandal and Palain.

I had always wanted to fish in the Mandal. Eventually, in mid-July 1996, armed with the permits I needed, I found myself at Rathuwadab on the banks of the river, at the northern periphery of the Reserve. Seventy-two-year old N. S. Negi, who worked in Corbett Tiger Reserve as a Senior Range Officer for nineteen years, accompanied his brother, J. S. Negi, and me. He had fished extensively in the Mandal River until twenty years earlier.

When we reached Rathuwadab, cottony clouds drifted over the emerald green forests. Paddy was being planted in the terraced fields. Lime-white water flowed rapidly in the river. All this indicated that the monsoon had set in the valley a few weeks ago. We were tempted to go fishing the same warm and sunny afternoon.

Mr N.S. Negi took us straight to the confluence of the Kateur and Mandal rivers where twenty years before, also in July, he had caught several fish weighing over ten kilograms. The confluence is about ten kilometres from Maidaban where the river enters the forest. Several boys were playing and swimming at the confluence and two of them had improvised fishing equipment. They had not caught any fish that day. They said that the largest they had caught this season weighed two kilograms. In spite of many attempts, with the best fishing gear available in the market, we had only one fish in the bag in the end, which weighed around 500 grams. We moved further up the river from pool to pool but all were empty. We met a fourteen year-old boy, adept at crossing the river to use his fishing gear. Seeing our disappointed faces, the boy told us why there were no fish. He said poachers set dynamite to kill fish almost every day from July to September. He added that the fish poachers had not come that day having heard of our trip.

By this time the sunlight was fading and the brain-fever bird started calling. In legend, this bird's mournful call is the cry of a girl calling out to a lost sister. Our gloom at hearing of dynamiting in a river that flows through a premier protected area, deepened with the bird's melancholic call. I had seen fish being massacred with dynamite in Garhwal and in Parambikulam. But I had been under the illusion that mahseer in Corbett Tiger Reserve was safe from such vandalism.

The next morning we drove along the river for thirteen kilometres to fish at the confluence of the Kali and Mandal rivers, far away from human habitation. The water in the Mandal was warm while that of the Kali, which springs out of a deep, well-wooded valley, was cold. In this serene setting appeared ten men who came up the river. We observed their ominous presence with bated breath. About two hundred metres away they dynamited a large deep pool with formidable rapidity. We rushed towards them but they melted away. Dead and dying fish drifted along the river. Although spots such as the confluence of two rivers are ideal fishing sites, the largest fish we caught weighed only about two kilograms. Corbett's giant mahseer seemed part of a mythical past, dynamited out of existence.

In the evening, on the lawn of the Rathuwadab rest house, we chatted with some village elders and the forest staff. One elderly man talked about the past abundance of fish between July and September. He said each household got sufficient oil for burning its lamps by smoking the fish. 'If my generation is well built, healthy and intelligent,' he went on, 'it is because we ate so much fish in our younger days for about three months every year.' Dynamiting, which kills even small fish, has apparently been going on for the last fifteen years and no one had thought it inhuman. We learnt that other mahseer spawning habitats—Palain and Ramganga—were also not safe from dynamiting. Fish in the Ramganga reservoir also suffered from illegal netting. In the pride of India's protected areas, Corbett National Park, the future of the mahseer, a protected species, looked deeply uncertain.

Even in Garhwal the story is much the same. From Jim Corbett's fishing accounts in *The Maneating Leopard of Rudraprayag* we know that in the past, large mahseer occurred in abundance even at Rudraprayag, the confluence of the Alaknanda and Mandakini, seventy kilometres upstream of Devprayag. Locals also report mahseer in the past in Nandprayag, the confluence of the Nandakini and Alaknanda, fifty kilometres upstream of Rudraprayag. Mahseer habitat was continuous till downstream of Rishikesh. But it was broken and altered by the construction of barrages in the early 1970s at Rishikesh and Haridwar, and by the Chilla power channel. The Gangetic system of the Garhwal Himalaya, with the Bhagirathi and Mandakini tributaries of the Ganga, has more than 250 kilometres of continuous habitat of immense potential. But even so, the situation here is alarming.

Back at Corbett National Park, we decided something urgently needed to be done. We were involved in a conservation initiative called 'Operation Eye of the Tiger' to save the tiger, its habitat and allied species. We decided to use this programme to forge a link between the people and the Forest Department and evolve a conservation programme to protect the mahseer when it comes to Mandal valley to spawn.

The plan would include giving waterproof clothing to the staff to enable them patrol even during the rains, and awards to those who control poaching. We called the women of Mandal valley for a meeting and explained the importance of mahseer for the health and growth of their children. We wanted the women's help in protecting the fish. We wanted to educate the young boys and men of the valley about the evils of dynamiting, while encouraging them to fish with line and casting net. Since the presence of sportsmen discourages illegal activities, we would encourage sports fishing with the permission of the Forest Department. Local NGOs would be enlisted to help in efforts to educate people to catch fish for sport and release them again in the waters.

Beyond the Mandal, on a larger scale in the Himalaya, the river stretch from Devprayag to Rishikesh, which has about a hundred kilometres of potential mahseer habitat, could be declared a sanctuary. We can try to curb the practice of using the Ganga and its tributaries as a garbage dump with the help of a trained and motivated guard force of local people. Tributaries like the Nayar river, according to Dr P. Nautiyal of Garhwal University, need special protection, as the mahseer young remain in it for a year before descending to the main river.

For mahseer to survive, whether in Parambikulam or the

Ramganga, the measures that need to be taken are much the same. People need to be convinced that fish is a renewable resource, but it cannot renew itself when it is being massacred thoughtlessly. Fishing the mahseer must be controlled for it to return even to a shadow of its old glory.

10   Tracking the Lions of Gir

One of the fast disappearing capabilities of people living in and around jungles is their ability to track and locate wild animals. The conservation community is weaning jungle inhabitants away from their traditional ways of living in order to reduce pressures on protected areas. But this blessing for animals comes at a human cost. When dependence on jungle-based livelihood is reduced, traditionally acquired jungle craft also disappears. While the efforts of the conservation community dilute pressures on forests, sadly, they also wash away skills based on physical fitness, and the ability to see, hear, smell, and then logically interpret signs in the jungle. One protected area in India where this skill is still being fostered, by tracking wild lions, is Gir in the state of Gujarat, the last bastion of the Asiatic lion. This hundred-year-old skill was probably promoted by the former Nawab of Junagadh to facilitate the hunting of lions.

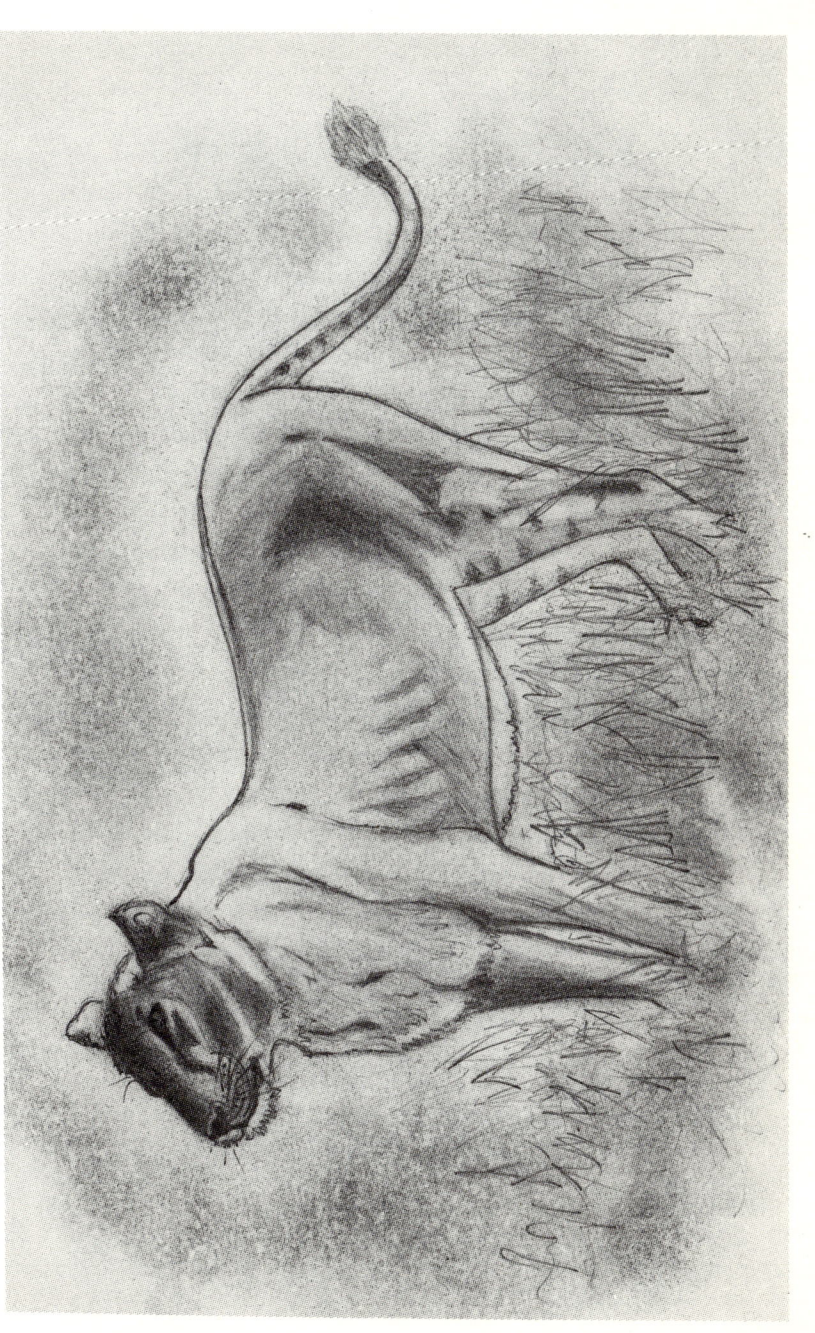

I tracked lions in 1995 with Dhanabai and Ibrahim, two of the many trackers employed by the Forest Department. Both had worked on projects of the Wildlife Institute of India in Gir for nearly six years. They were hard-working, trustworthy and fearless. Dhanabai even fought a male lion in May 1990 to save the life of an officer he had accompanied into the forest during a lion census. The officer had approached a mating pair to photograph them, not heeding Dhanabhai's repeated warnings. The officer had not realised that mating lions could be aggressive and approaching them on foot is dangerous. Luckily, the lion ran away as Dhanabhai rained powerful punches on its face. The officer's folly caused Dhanabai to spend several weeks in hospital.

When we set out from Sasan, the tourism headquarters in western Gir, the pale crescent of the moon hung in an eastern sky which glowed orange in the rising sun. Stars, fading in the aura of the approaching light, powdered the sky. News of recent sightings helps one decide where to go to track lions. In this case, the sighting of a group of three adult females and six nine-month-old cubs by the trackers the previous day helped us to decide the area we would head for. The lions had been seen near Raidi, about eight kilometres north-east of Sasan, at an abandoned cattle camp of the *maldharis*, a local pastoral community. It is much easier to locate lions when they are on the move during the cool hours of the day, as prey animals such as deer and peafowl unfailingly sound alarm calls at the sight of large predators. The alarm calls can indicate the location of the lions.

Reaching Raidi, we decided to walk along the road to locate pugmarks that would provide clues about the direction the lions had gone in. The glow in the eastern sky had become paler and alarm calls of the chital rang out a kilometre north of us as we started walking along the road.

Soon we discovered that the lions had not walked along that road the previous night and therefore we had to track them from the place where they had been seen the previous day. We walked through the forest, observing the habitat quality of Gir. The tree vegetation was dominated by bher (*Zizyphus mauritiana*) which was fruiting in abundance. Under many trees the ground was literally matted with its yellow and red ripe berries. It serves as the staple diet of wild ungulates in Gir in winter. In summer, the fallen leaves of bher provide their protein requirements. The grass, which had dried and was golden yellow in colour, was a metre tall in most places. *Apluda mutica*, a nutritious fodder grass, dominated the grass community. Weeds like *lantana* and *eupatorium*, which are common in most other protected areas in the country, were very rare here.

One surprising aspect of the trailing was that the trackers were not silent. On the contrary, they talked loudly, joked, and occasionally loudly called '*drruu-drruu-drruu*'. This is the call trackers make when they approach lions with bait, usually a buffalo calf. This noisy approach is for safety: it alerts the lions, which respond with a soft growl and lashing of the tail. Resting in the dry undergrowth, lions can remain exceedingly well camouflaged, and a sudden or very close approach to those either at fresh kills or with cubs can be dangerous. Traditionally, trackers carry either a strong 1.5 metre stick or a small axe while trailing lions.

I was also amazed by the ability of the trackers to observe signs of the lion on the sun-baked earth—broken grass, bent grass, crushed dry teak leaves, upturned stones and even fresh scat in the dense leaf-litter. All these clues indicated the direction in which the lions had gone. The tracks of the lions went over a ridge towards the revenue lands where the village Surat Ghad is situated. My trackers informed me that the Raidi pride got close to seventy-five per cent of its prey—buffaloes and cattle—from the villages, because wild ungulates were scarce in the forest periphery in which they hunted. This certainly seemed true that morning: during our twelve-kilometre search, through all sorts of vegetation types and across varied terrain, we encountered only one group of nilgai, three in number. We did, however, see about sixty buffaloes and cattle, in three herds, accompanied by graziers.

One strategy during tracking was seeking information from the cattle graziers about the whereabouts of the lions. All the three graziers told us that they had not heard the roar of lions the previous evening. Though we failed to see any fresh signs of lions, we saw fresh tracks of leopard and hyena in several places. Besides lion, the high density of leopard and hyena is another significant conservation value of Gir.

Though late December is about the coldest winter can get, by eleven in the morning it became exceedingly hot. As lions usually seek shade at such times, it becomes difficult to locate them and therefore we abandoned the search. At around three, I was informed that a group of three adult females and two cubs had been seen by a group of tourists crossing the road in the morning on the way to Raidi. We drove upto the point where the lions had been seen and then followed the trail on foot. The early afternoon was much warmer than the forenoon, and dust, which had probably been wet in the morning, flew from the bushes as we walked through the forest now. Peafowl feeding on the bher fruits flew helter skelter as we surprised them. Soon the tracks led us to Thapli nallah, which had water oozing from many places in the stream bed, dense vegetation and abundant ungulate signs. In the nallah, we came across the place where the group of lions had rested. Chital alarm calls from different directions confused us about where to go next and we called it a day as light started fading from the forest.

Early the next morning, as we were debating the day's exercise, we got a message that lions near Chhataria had killed three cows five kilometres west of Sasan. The sun had risen over the hills when we began tracking. The trackers were not sure whether the cattle had been killed by the Raidi or Devalia group which had three adult females and three eight-month-old cubs. The kills had been made on a hill slope. The valley, where the lions were likely to have retired after gorging on the kills, was overgrown with *Acacia nilotica*, a thorn tree, and dense tall grass. Therefore, though the search was for a short duration, all of us got sufficient exercise as we went along animal paths through dense bushes, often on our knees.

As we crawled through the undergrowth, a lioness which was resting amidst the grass raised her head, growled and lashed her tail vigorously on the ground. She was twenty metres away and had she remained silent, we would have gone past, oblivious to her presence. When we stopped advancing she remained still and silent and watched us intently. Only the black of her eyes, mouth and tip of the tail were distinguishable from the wheat-brown dry grass around. There was a large cub sleeping nearby; the rest of the pride could not be seen. Both the lions had distended bellies, which indicated that they had eaten to the full. As we watched, the lioness went to sleep. With such full bellies and the increasing warmth of the day there was very little chance that they would move out of the cover during the day. Therefore, we returned to Sasan.

In Sasan I was told about a sambar kill which had been made by a solitary prime adult male in the river Chhodia, five kilometres east of Sasan, four days before. Mohammed, the tracker who had located the kill earlier, found it again with ease. The lion had killed the sambar in the river bed, had eviscerated it hardly five metres from the place where it was killed, and had then dragged it into a tangle of creepers and climbers in the dense and cool riverine forest. Fresh tracks of a leopard were all around the lion tracks.

The hard antlers of the stag measuring 28 inches and sharp teeth on its lower jaw indicated that it was a prime young animal, about four years old. The lion had probably eaten at least 120 kilograms of meat during the four days it was with the kill. It was likely that a leopard had come to scavenge on the remains.

A four-year study on the lions of Gir by the Wildlife Institute of India, using radio-telemetry, had concluded that a significant portion of the diet of the seemingly slow adult male lions comes from livestock. We had recommended therefore that the programme to settle the maldharis and their buffaloes outside Gir should be carried out in a phased manner, over a period of twenty-odd years, so that the new generation of male lions would develop the ability to hunt wild ungulates and switch their diet gradually. We had, however, recommended this with the nagging question at the back of our minds about whether the adult male lions would ever be able to live life without depending much on livestock. The scene at Chhodia suggested the possibility.

Is lion-tracking a redundant skill in modern times or does it have any uses? Several benefits came to my mind. It gives the wildlife staff an excellent opportunity to know their area thoroughly. Walking through the bush looking for lions may be the best way of patrolling and warding off illegal activities like snaring, rampant in many protected areas throughout the country. The tracking programme keeps the staff physically fit and makes them proficient in jungle craft, all vital for wildlife personnel. This programme, therefore, needs to be extended to all of Gir so that all the staff benefits from it. If observations made during tracking, as in Chhodia, were carefully recorded, our knowledge of this critically endangered subspecies—knowledge vital for planning suitable conservation measures—would improve dramatically.

Tracking can also help generate some revenue for conservation in Gir. Several wildlife enthusiasts would be willing to pay a generous fee for the first hand experience of tracking lions in the traditional way. Without any disturbance to the habitat and the lions a minimum of a hundred trips can be permitted in a year. A major portion of the revenue generated can be added to the 'Gir Welfare Fund' which aims at providing support measures to the poorly paid staff.

One of the most tangible benefits of this tracking programme is that it enables the Forest Department to show the lions to visitors who are very keen to observe this magnificent felid in its natural setting. The intense look of a lion through a dense mat of grass, its low growl and the lashing of its tail warning the visitor not to take any further liberties with its pride, is a memorable experience. Visitors who are fortunate enough to observe the lion in its natural setting are likely to become friends of wildlife and champions of conservation.